Meyer Levin

Twayne's United States Authors Series

TUSAS 406

MEYER LEVIN
(1905–1981)
Photo Credit: Mikael Levin

Meyer Levin

By Steven J. Rubin
University of South Florida

Twayne Publishers • Boston

Meyer Levin

Steven J. Rubin

Published by Twayne Publishers
A Division of G. K. Hall & Company
70 Lincoln Street
Boston, Massachusetts 02111

Book production by John Amburg
Book design by Barbara Anderson

Printed on permanent/durable
acid-free paper and bound in
The United States of America.

Library of Congress Cataloging in Publication Data

Rubin, Steven J.
Meyer Levin.

(Twayne's United States authors series ; TUSAS 406)
Bibliography: p. 158
Includes index.
1. Levin, Meyer, 1905–1981—Criticism and
interpretation. I. Title. II. Series.
PS3523.E7994Z87 813'.52 81–23327
ISBN 0–8057–7335–5 AACR2

For my Mother and Father

Contents

About the Author

Steven J. Rubin is an associate professor and associate chairman of the Department of English at the University of South Florida. He received his Ph.D. in comparative literature from the University of Michigan in 1969. Dr. Rubin has taught English and foreign languages at the University of South Florida, the Institute for American Universities, Aix-en-Provence, France, and the Institut d'Anglais Charles V, University of Paris VII. In 1979 he was the recipient of a Fulbright-Hays Award under the auspices of the Franco-American Commission for Educational Exchange. Dr. Rubin has published numerous articles in the fields of comparative and ethnic studies in such journals as *Studies in American Jewish Literature*, the *Journal of Ethnic Studies, Studies in Short Fiction, Africa Report, International Fiction Review,* and *Studies in Black Literature.* He is a member of the Editorial Advisory Board of MELUS (the journal of the Society for the Study of the Multi-Ethnic Literature of the United States).

Preface

The literary achievement of Meyer Levin includes more than twenty-five volumes. In the course of a career which spanned almost six decades, Levin was a novelist, filmmaker, dramatist, critic, and historian. Although his career suffered numerous and sometimes unexplained setbacks, Levin's reputation as a writer is well established. This judgment is not based solely on longevity or high productivity. Many of his works have been commercially successful: some of his novels have sold well, and several have been translated into various languages. Yet critical and scholarly recognition has not been forthcoming. For the most part he is given only cursory treatment in studies and anthologies of American Jewish literature, and he is rarely mentioned in wider treatments of American fiction. There exist no full-length analyses of his work and very few critical articles. What criticism has appeared, is often misleading or irrelevant, frequently concentrating on Levin's personal difficulties, his legal problems, or his political views, rather than on his literary achievement.

It is difficult to understand the total lack of scholarly interest in Levin's work. To be sure, many of his novels suffer needless lapses in style; many are lengthy and verbose. Others, however, like *The Old Bunch, Citizens*, and *Compulsion*, are worthy of critical attention.

My purpose throughout this study will be to provide a clear critical analysis of Levin's fiction and to evaluate his role in the development of American Jewish literature. As a Jewish author, Levin belonged to a generation of writers who wrote of the difficult problems of assimilation and ethnic identity at a time when these themes were not fashionable in American literature. The shortened careers of many of Levin's contemporaries—Daniel

Fuchs, Mike Gold, and Henry Roth, for example—provide dramatic testimony to this fact. Yet Levin was part of a social and literary process that culminated in the achievements of such talented writers as Saul Bellow, Bernard Malamud, and Philip Roth. Moreover, Levin's novels and stories are interesting and significant enough to justify extended criticism.

Levin wrote two autobiographical works: *In Search* (1950) and *The Obsession* (1973). I have relied on these, several published interviews, and my own conversations with Mr. Levin, to provide an outline of the major events of his life and to analyze the the importance of those events to his work and thought, especially as they relate to his early struggle to define his uncertain Jewish identity.

I have quoted extensively from Levin's fiction in order to familiarize the reader with material that is generally not well-known. I have also included a brief plot summary of each work so as to orient the reader to the critical discussion of characters, themes, and techniques that follows. In most cases, I have examined the works chronologically in order to provide a coherent and logical approach to a wide diversity of subjects and themes. The exceptions to this are *The Obsession*, which is discussed as part of Levin's involvement with *The Diary of Anne Frank*, and several short stories which are examined in the last chapter on Levin and Israel.

I am grateful for having had the opportunity to have discussed Mr. Levin's career with him personally and candidly. I would also like to express my appreciation to the Department of English at the University of South Florida for providing research time during the preparation of the manuscript. I am indebted to my colleagues Jean Moore and Edgar Hirshberg for reading parts of the manuscript and for the helpful suggestions they offered. Finally, my sincere gratitude to Elizabeth Melton for her efficient typing of the manuscript.

STEVEN J. RUBIN

University of South Florida

Chronology

1905 Meyer Levin born 8 October in Chicago, Illinois, to Joseph and Golda Levin.

1924 Works for the *Chicago Daily News.* Graduates from the University of Chicago. February, "Roosevelt Road: Three Chicago Sketches" published in *Menorah Journal.*

1924–1925 Studies in Paris with Fernand Léger. Travels in Europe. First trip to Palestine.

1925–1926 Works for the *Chicago Evening America.* Works as Cultural Director at Chicago's Jewish People's Institute.

1927 Second trip to Palestine. Works for six months on Yagur kibbutz near Haifa.

1929 *Reporter,* first novel.

1930 *Frankie and Johnny.*

1931 *Yehuda.*

1932 *The Golden Mountain* (*Classic Hassidic Tales*).

1933 Marries Mable Schamp. *The New Bridge.* Associate editor and film critic for *Esquire.*

1937 *The Old Bunch.*

1937–1938 Travels to Spain as a war correspondent. Third trip to Palestine.

1940 *Citizens.*

1941–1943 Joins the Office of War Information as writer-director-producer of documentary films. Works for the U.S. Psychological Warfare division. Divorced. Joins Psychological Warfare Division in London.

1944–1945 War correspondent for the Jewish Telegraphic Agency and the Overseas News Agency, reporting on Hitler's concentration camps.

1947	Films *My Father's House* in Palestine. *My Father's House.*
1947–1948	Works with the *Haganah* (Jewish underground) in the illegal emigration of Jews to Palestine. Films *The Illegals* and *Voyage of the Unafraid.*
1948	Marries novelist Tereska Torres, daughter of sculptor Marek Szwarc in Paris.
1950	*In Search.*
1952	Dramatization of Anne Frank's *The Diary of a Young Girl.*
1953	Court battle for production rights.
1956	*Compulsion.*
1959	*Compulsion, A Play. Eva.* Residence in Herzlia on Sea, Israel.
1963	*The Fanatic.*
1965	*The Stronghold.*
1968	*Gore and Igor.*
1972	*The Settlers.*
1973	*The Obsession.*
1974	*The Spell of Time.*
1978	*The Harvest.*
1981	Died 9 July in Jerusalem, Israel. *The Architect.*

Chapter One
Introduction

Family Background and Early Years

Meyer Levin was born on 8 October 1905 in the Jewish neighborhood of Chicago's West Side. His immigrant parents, Joseph and Golda Levin had come to this country at the turn of the century from the Vilna area of Russia. In his autobiography, *In Search* (1950), Levin recalled that his father was a tailor "with a hole-in-the-wall shop near the old Dearborn Station, downtown." Although the Levins were not prosperous, the older Levin managed, doing "pressing and mending, and a little buying and selling of used clothing, work tools, and odds and ends possessed by South State Street derelicts."[1]

The Levin family lived in the vicinity of Chicago's Racine Avenue. Like many ethnic urban neighborhoods at the beginning of the century, the area was rapidly changing in identity as one group of immigrants climbed up the socioeconomic ladder and out of the ghetto to be replaced by another. By the turn of the century, the Jews of Chicago had supplanted the Irish and, as Meyer Levin was growing up, the Italians were in the process of replacing the Jews. The procedure was rarely harmonious. Racine Avenue marked an uneasy divide: one side was Jewish, the other Italian. Many years later Levin described his daily walk to school as a precarious journey through enemy territory: "On Racine Avenue, our side was still Jewish, but the Italians faced us from across the street. From our house to the corner we felt nearly safe, but once we turned into Taylor Street on the way to the Andrew Jackson School, we were in entirely Italian territory. The first place of refuge was a friendly Italian's grocery store. . . . Then, after peering out to make sure the coast was clear, we would scuttle the rest of the way to school" (7). For the child of immigrant parents, growing up Jewish was not an easy experience. "My dominant childhood memory," Levin later claimed "is of fear and shame at being a Jew" (5).

By the time he had reached the upper grades of the Andrew Jackson School, the neighborhood was virtually all Italian, and Levin felt more than ever a sense of estrangement: "We children believed ourselves to be smarter than the wops. Yet they seemed more American. For though the Italians were immigrants just like our parents, their children already seemed to have a native right over us, a right to call us sheenie and kike which had overtones of degradation far beyond anything associated with wop or dago" (6).

Only a handful of Jewish children remained in Levin's school, and those that did attended a Hebrew class in the old and all but deserted Jewish People's Institute that still functioned in the neighborhood. Here he studied not only the Hebrew language but also Jewish history, folklore, and culture. Despite his "fear and shame" of being somehow different and non-American, the ancient tales of his ancestors thrilled and fascinated him. The curious mixture which was to mark his future life and work, the fusion—as he later stated—of "Chicago and Chassidism," had begun to form.

As a precocious youth still in the Andrew Jackson School, Levin began writing poems and learning the workings of the school's print shop. By the time he entered high school, he had already launched a literary career of sorts by writing stories for the school magazine, which was to eventually come under his editorship. At the time another Jew, Ben Hecht, whose sketches entitled "A Thousand and One Afternoons in Chicago" appeared in the *Chicago Daily News*, was the local literary idol. To an aspiring writer, Hecht—and his counterpart at the *News*, Maxwell Bodenheim—were models to be revered and emulated. While still in high school, Levin sent a Hecht-like sketch of life on the West Side to the great man. Within a week Levin received a terse, but optimistic reply. "You can write," pronounced Hecht. No greater encouragement could have served the young writer better.

Levin entered the University of Chicago at the early age of sixteen. He immediately began to move in the literary circles of the university, enrolling in the writing class of the then well-known novelist, James Weber Linn. Along with another beginning author, John Gunther, Levin formed a literary magazine, *The Circle*, which became the starting point in the careers of several young Chicago writers.

During the time Levin and Gunther were at the university, many Chicagoans believed their city to be at the center of the American literary tradition. The book page of the *Chicago Daily News*, for example, proclaimed the city to be the literary capital of America. Many of the great writers of the early part of the century were associated with Chicago: Dreiser, Sandberg, Edgar Lee Masters, Vachel Lindsay, Harriet Monroe, Floyd Dell, and, of course, Hecht and Bodenheim. Many of these authors had worked at various points in their careers for the *Chicago Daily News*. For an aspiring writer there was no better place to start than the *News*. "One's development as a writer," Levin recalled, "required an apprenticeship on the *News*. . . . In those days one didn't apply for a newspaper job in order to become a journalist. At least, not on the *Chicago Daily News*. One applied in order to become an author. A reporter's job was merely a way of earning a living while one 'wrote' " (17–18).

With the help of Hecht's recommendation, Levin secured a part-time job at the *News* as a picture chaser, the traditional starting place on the paper. From there he moved to campus reporter and eventually to feature writer. It was here that Levin covered the most sensational story of the decade, the Leopold-Loeb murder case and trial, which was to become many years later the subject of his best known work, *Compulsion*.

In the meantime, Levin was continuing his literary activities at the University of Chicago, taking courses in writing and composing stories for *The Circle*. As a result of the success of these pieces, he received a letter from the editor of a magazine called *Menorah Journal*—a journal of Jewish cultural life that was eventually to become *Commentary*—asking him to submit material. Several of his sketches of Chicago's West Side were accepted. For Levin, however, publication in the *Menorah Journal* represented a rather limited success. The journal and its readers were almost exclusively Jewish, and Levin wanted more than ever to prove himself as an "American" author.

At an age when most students were only beginning college, Levin graduated from the University of Chicago and immediately set off for Europe. The year was 1924, and this was the requisite journey for aspiring writers and artists: "This was the high period of American expatriates in Paris. We knew we had to go to the Café Dome, study art and practice sex" (24).

While in Paris Levin briefly studied painting with the well-known artist Fernand Léger and the less renowned Marek Szwarc. Of the two it was Szwarc who was to have a lasting influence on Levin's life and work. Through the example of Szwarc, Levin began to understand the rich and imaginative possibilities of an art form conceived within a religious framework. Whereas Levin had always associated religious traditionalism with the immigrant ways of his parents' generation (the "greenhorns" of Chicago), Szwarc used the legends and figures of the past to enhance his art and to give it universal meaning. His work often pictured old-world Polish Jews with long coats, beards, and earlocks. But instead of pathetic misfits, these Jews were portrayed as possessing a timeless dignity and pride. For Levin—a young American still struggling with the ambiguities of his Jewish identity—the effect was startling: "They were the people of my immediate past, now viewed as worthy ancestors rather than as ridiculous long-beards. I didn't know yet how profoundly this realization was stirring within me, and that something within me required that I go all the way back to find out where I came from" (26). Although it was to be several years before Levin was able to effectively integrate his sense of a Jewish past with his creative present, it was through this early association with Marek Szwarc that he began to realize "that it was appropriate for a Jewish artist to occupy himself with the material of Jewish life, that he need not feel ashamed of it, need not feel that it was limiting, need not feel that it was of minor value" (24).

After almost a year of living and studying in Paris, Levin left to continue his European odyssey, wandering through Vienna, Italy, and Greece. Although he had an impulse to go on to Poland and discover his parents' village near Vilna, he resisted. He was, as he later admitted, "perhaps afraid." Yet the notion of the importance of the Jewish past and of the future fate of world Jewry was not to leave him. Eventually Levin journeyed to Palestine, partly out of curiosity, and partly because the editor of *Menorah Journal* had written to him suggesting an assignment to cover the opening of the Hebrew University in Jerusalem. At the time, Levin, like most of his American contemporaries, was not a Zionist. During the 1920s Zionism was rarely an issue of any significance with the great majority of American Jews. If it was discussed at all, it was done in the Yiddish press and was of interest primarily to Jews from the old country. Levin's interest in the mandate of Palestine, at this point in his career, was mostly academic.

His trip lasted only several weeks, but the impression the land and its people made on the young author was intense: "The experience of Palestine was electrifying. I felt like a discoverer. Here were Jews like early Americans, riding guard at night in vigilance against hostile natives, pioneering in the malarial marshes, and living in communal groups. . . . I was possessed by the physical beauty of the land, so deeply moved that I began to wonder whether my reactions were not instinct with racial memory. . . . I felt an overwhelming rightness of place" (27). The experience never left him. Several years later Levin was able to write of Palestine in somewhat less romantic, yet equally optimistic terms. *Yehuda* (1931) was the first novel about kibbutz life in the English language.[2] Four decades after the publication of *Yehuda*,

Levin wrote his most definitive works on the subject of Zionism and the history of Israel. *The Settlers* (1972) and its sequel, *The Harvest* (1978) record the settlement of the promised land from the beginning of the century through the founding of the independent state of Israel.

Levin was to return many times to Palestine. In 1925, however, he did not linger long. His strong feeling of identification with his Jewish origins and with the idea of peoplehood confused and frightened him: his home was Chicago, and his future was as an "American" writer. Accordingly, he returned to his native city and began working as a reporter for the Hearst *Chicago Evening American*. During his free time, he turned his efforts to fiction. The results of this period were several short stories and two early novels: *Reporter* (1929) and *Frankie and Johnny* (1930). The novels contained little indication of the author's preoccupation with the question of Jewish identity. The stories, however, which were written for *Menorah Journal,* were self-consciously Jewish and reveal Levin's early need to dramatize the other, Jewish side of his personality.

Early Short Stories

Levin's first published efforts consisted of short stories and sketches of Jewish life which appeared throughout the 1920s in *Menorah Journal.* "Three Chicago Sketches" was published in the February 1924 issue of the magazine. Levin probably based his idea for these sketches of Chicago's West Side on Ben Hecht's "A Thousand and One Afternoons in Chicago," which was appearing at the time in the *Chicago Daily News.* The first, "Molasses Tide," an impressionistic portrait of Chicago's Roosevelt Road, is written in a style that is self-consciously and overly metaphorical: "Roosevelt Road is a treadmill over which pass beasts. Beasts of many kinds pass back and forth . . . back and forth. . . . The stream of beasts becomes like a flow of molasses. Drops of molasses escape from the stream and trickle into big white lights."[3] Although the language seems forced and affected, "Molasses Tide" is an interesting early effort and an effective abstract vision of a busy Chicago street, its people, and its activities. In his attempt to create a language that would metaphorically render the pulsing life of the city, Levin's style is somewhat similar to the impressionistic prose of such writers as Jean Toomer and Hart Crane, who also began their careers around this time. "Molasses Tide," however, is not a part of a larger, more comprehensive work. Standing alone, it only hints at a more complete symbolic structure and a more meaningful interpretation.

The second sketch, "Around the Soap-Box," takes a more realistic look at the people who frequent Sunday soapbox debates. Among those present are "A cloak shop worker who spent his time reading philosophy . . . a man who quoted Hebrew from the Bible . . . Aronson the atheist" (48). These as well as various salesmen, tailors, and machinists spend their afternoons discussing religion, evolution, the inevitability of death, agnosticism, and communism. Although there is nothing unusual or particularly skillful in this sketch, Levin does suceed in rendering the inner mood of the place, as well as the frantic activity that is a part of Sunday afternoon in the park.

The last piece, "Cheuing Gohm" (Chewing Gum), in spite of Levin's unnecessary use of phonic translation in the title, is the most effective and the most complete of the three. The story portrays an old Jewish immigrant who tries to earn a meager living by peddling chewing gum in his adopted country. The New World, however, is a strange and foreign place, its language all but incomprehensible to him. His vision has begun to fail, and he can no longer successfully compete with the younger, more aggressive vendors who have taken over his territory. Although somewhat melodramatic, Levin's portrayal of the immigrant experience is effective. In this very short but moving piece Levin succeeds in conveying the tragedy and disillusion of those who journeyed to the New World with inflated dreams only to find loneliness, isolation, and poverty. His blind chewing gum vendor embodies all that the immigrant hoped for and all that failed: "And he drifts on, singing the magic cry of the new world that he can neither see nor understand: 'Cheuing Gohm . . . Cheuing Gohm . . . Cheuing Gohm . . .' " (51).

Several months after the appearance of "Three Chicago Sketches," *Menorah Journal* published Levin's short story "A Seder." The theme, which was to dominate much of American Jewish writing several decades later, explores the alienation of the new generation of secular Jews from the traditions and symbols of their past. "A Seder" is the story of a Jewish family and their feeble attempt to celebrate the first night of Passover. Preoccupied and self-absorbed, the members of the Berger family remain isolated from each other and estranged from their religion. A teenage daughter wants to go to the latest movie with her friends; Mrs. Berger can think only of the petty annoyances and difficulties of her quotidian existence. Mendell Berger, the father, ineffectual as the head of the family, passively sits and remembers more meaningful Passovers in the old country. Through a series of flashbacks, Levin gives his readers a view of a more peaceful and harmonious existence in Mendell Berger's boyhood European town. Juxtaposed against the beauty and serenity of this vision is the picture of the impersonal, stark, urban night which seems to surround the Berger apartment: "A jumble of rear walls and side walls of three story flat buildings. . . . The buildings outlined themselves against the sky, as if they had been cut by a child out of black paper and pasted against blue cardboard."[4] The imagery, purposely flat and somber, reflects the lonely and disaffected condition of Mendell Berger and his generation. Like the chewing gum vendor, he is separated from his old-world roots but has failed to establish a firm or comfortable footing in his new country. The adjustment to a different society and the modern world of America will come, Levin suggests, with the next generation. That generation, however, represented as it is by the morose and self-centered Berger children, seems to offer little hope for the future of American Judaism.

Although these early stories and sketches were successful in tone and characterization, Levin viewed his debut into the published world with misgivings: "I felt a slight uneasiness that my first serious acceptance should be in what I considered a limited world, for all I wrote seemed to flow into this side channel."[5] The investigation of Jewish themes and characters was somehow associated in his mind with a lesser talent and a parochial vision. Accordingly, Levin's next efforts—two rather undistinguished novels—purposely avoided the issue of Jewish identity.

Chapter Two

Early Fiction: The Divided Self

In a 1947 article in *Commentary*, Levin, by then a well-known figure in American Jewish letters, stated: "I am a writer who from his beginnings tried to express himself as an American Jew."[1] Although this might be true of his early sketches and stories, Levin could not, in all truth, lay claim to giving literary expression to his ethnic identity early in his career. Although such a possibility certainly occurred to him, Levin was unable or unwilling to discuss the theme of Jewish identity in his early novels. On the contrary, his first thought as a young writer was to purge his work of any trace of ethnicity, partly out of a certain ambivalence of his own, partly out of practical considerations: "You couldn't successfully write about Jews for the American market," Levin claimed. "I tried to erase what was Jewish in my characters."[2]

Levin's early perception of the realities of the commercial market was correct. Although the Jewish community could boast of such talented writers as Ludwig Lewisohn, Anzia Yerzierska, Samuel Ornitz, Abraham Cahan, and Mary Antin—all of whom wrote movingly of the first generation of American Jews—the commercial success of early American Jewish literature was limited. Nor did things improve for the second generation Jewish writers of the 1930s. Michael Gold's *Jews Without Money* (1930) sold relatively well, but Henry Roth's masterpiece *Call It Sleep* (1934) sold only four thousand copies. And the sale of Daniel Fuch's three novels about Jewish life in Brooklyn—*Summer in Williamsburg* (1934), *Homage to Blenholt* (1936), and *Low*

Company (1937)—was even lower: 400, 400, and 1,200 copies respectively.[3] Themes of Jewish life were not in vogue during the first half of the century, and undoubtably the careers of even the most successful Jewish writers suffered as a result. Bernard Sherman, in *The Invention of the Jew*, concludes that although there is some evidence to the contrary, "the truth of the matter seems to be that prior to the late 1950s, novels of Jewish life were not enthusiastically received, although several hundred were published."[4]

Aware of these realities, and not yet feeling the urgency to explore the subtle ambiguities of his own Jewishness, Levin patterned his literary efforts to what he believed to be the mainstream of contemporary American fiction. He took his early themes and subjects not from the Jewish ghettos of New York or Chicago, but rather from the Jazz Age world of Hemingway and Fitzgerald. In both *Reporter* and *Frankie and Johnny*, character, situation, and theme are carefully drawn so as to reveal little or nothing of the author's Jewishness. So great was Levin's uncertainty toward his own identity, so great was his need to be accepted as an ecumenical author, that the issues associated with Jewish life, which were to play so great a role in his future personal and artistic endeavors, could be approached in only the most indirect manner.

Reporter

"As soon as I returned to Chicago," Levin recalled in his autobiography, "I began to plan my literary career. First, I had to write a book" (28). The book, entitled *Reporter* (1929), was written shortly after Levin's return to the United States, and published by the John Day Company. Unfortunately, and in spite of Levin's desire to succeed as a novelist, *Reporter* remains an undistinguished first effort.

In an attempt to capture the emotional content and the inner reality of the events of the day, Levin conceived of a documentary novel in a journalistic style: "I had an idea for a book. It concerned the relationship of printed news—the appearance of things—to the reality of events. This was not so much a search for the 'news behind the news' as a wish to somehow render the fluidity of experience that became lost in the arid little paragraphs of newspaper stories. It seemed to me that if I could put down precisely what happened, down to the most trivial of events, I would inevitably capture reality" (28). Despite Levin's contention that he had conceived "perhaps the first" documentary novel, one that "stemmed from Joyce and Gertrude Stein," *Reporter* fails to adhere to even the most rudimentary demands of its genre. There is no development of character: people come and go with little justification or explanation. The novel contains neither plot nor internal structure but is rather a loosely connected series of random events.

The style is meant to be that of a reporter on his beat. Headlines appear at the top of each page in the manner of Dos Passos: "Bryan to Defy Darwin," "Lovers Die in Suicide Pact," "Five Dead in Gas Leak." Pages are often set in double columns to reflect the novel's newspaper format. Words run together, presumably to create the frantic atmosphere of the newsroom: "cmere" takes the place of "come here," for instance, as does "cityed" for "city editor"; and there are frequent uses of such colloquialisms as "y'know," "nope," "yup," and "ohmygod." Contemporary expressions such as "hot diggity," "chickie," and "dinkus" appear on almost every page. The language—made up largely of exaggerated Jazz Age jargon—renders much of the narrative puerile: "Chickie was Dinky's pet mulatto, fiery as hot tamales, and peppy as pluto water. When Chickie did the Charleston, naked on that table . . . Owow!"[5]

Levin's journalistic technique and the character of the reporter himself is reminiscent, as Allen Guttmann points out, of the young Hemingway: "One assumes the book was typed with shirtsleeves folded, with tie loosened, with cigarette at the side of the mouth, and with Ernest Hemingway of the *Toronto Star* clearly in mind."[6] Levin's style is, at times, minimal: "At 3 p.m. the temp. was 93. Tied the record for the last 23 years for 3 p.m. temp. on that date. If it reached 94 within an hour the 23 yr. record would be broken" (165). But more often he is given to flights of impressionistic and alliterative fancy: "Now while this flurry attained its highest fury and crayon, pencil, notes, phone books, flew through the sniffling air, now while the rewrite men did duck and gurgle, fling and dodge, scoop and tear and scrap in one wild burst of howling glorious glee, the very clever reporter sportively typed swiftly, pulled sheet from machine and halt-yelling handed it across the desks" (169). The language, moreover, is often exaggerated, sentimental, and overly metaphorical. An Italian is described as "juicy-fat"; a woman's breasts are "distant snow caps"; and eyes are not merely green, but "green as the cold green of seaweed."

The plot of the novel is inconsequential, as we follow the various news of the day: an interview with Clarence Darrow, the death of the president of the University of Chicago, the murder of mobster Vittorio Manfredi, graduation ceremonies, and a multitude of other events. Levin's protagonist is a newspaper reporter, but he appears only at scattered intervals, and there is little connection between events and characterization. The reader comes to learn nothing of the hero's personality or inner development. As a result, Levin's attempt to "capture reality" rarely moves beyond superficial observation.

The novel does, however, demonstrate Levin's ability to tell a story. Several of the book's episodes are interesting and dramatic on their own and probably would have been more successful if published as short sketches in the manner of those done earlier in *Menorah Journal.* One such "minidrama," entitled "Mildred 16, Kept From Paul, Drowns Self After Tryst," is told more from the reporter's own imagination than from his actual knowledge of the facts—for he can only speculate as to the emotions and events that motivated the young girl's suicide. The story is both moving and tragic, understated and well told, and is a good indication of what Levin could have achieved in *Reporter* had he not struggled to be technically original and innovative.

Reporter gives little indication of Levin's preoccupation with the role of the Jew in America. Interestingly, however, the novel is not without mention of Jews and Judaism. The book's protagonist is Jewish, although this fact is given little significance. Levin attempts to be "objective" in his mention of anything Jewish, but his authorial stance is often strangely anti-Semitic. A Jewish man at a Kiwanis Club luncheon, for example, is described disdainfully as a "loose-faced, paunch bellied Hebrew" (217). A woman at a neighborhood catastrophe is portrayed with equal dislike as a "dumpy, . . . busybody Jewish neighbor" (331). Levin's attempts at objectivity, therefore become paradoxically a type of self-hatred that reveals his early uncertainty toward his own Jewish identity. The relationship between the novel's protagonist and the author is obvious, as Levin himself readily admitted: "Reading the book in later years, I felt it was though I had been afraid to commit myself. There was an episode, for instance, in which he [the reporter] talked to a blatantly anti-Semitic lawyer, and during the interview I had the reporter wondering whether he shouldn't say out loud, 'by the way, I'm a Jew.' It was as though I myself had been struggling with this question all through the book."[7]

Levin's self-doubt in terms of his Jewish identity, the inability to resolve the basic dichotomy of his life, was to continue for many years. In the early 1930s there were subsequent efforts to explore the totally Jewish aspects of his personality. His second novel, however, contained no hint of the author's religion and was an even more obvious attempt by the young author to enter the contemporary American world of Jazz Age fiction.

Frankie and Johnny

Even before *Reporter*'s short-lived publication (the book was withdrawn from the bookstands several weeks after it appeared due to the threat of a lawsuit by a woman who thought she recognized herself in the novel), Levin had started work on his second novel. A story of young love, the events of *Frankie and Johnny* (1930) were loosely based on an incident in Levin's own life. In the novel, however, all mention of Jewishness, in any form, was avoided: "I tried to erase what was Jewish in my characters, to present them as a typical couple of young Americans. . . . My one desire was that my book be considered American."[8]

Frankie and Johnny depicts the growth and ultimate failure of young love set against the harsh and impersonal urban surroundings of Chicago. While still obviously the work of a maturing artist, the novel sustains considerably more emotion and credibility than *Reporter*. The book's defects are obvious: a lack of strong or interesting characterization, pretentious use of language, and a narrative that is overly long and verbose. Yet Levin's story of urban youth and their initiation into the adult world is nevertheless realistic and, at times, forceful.

The novel opens with Johnny's first encounter with Frances, the younger sister of his best friend, Steve. Frankie is in high school, and Johnny is holding his first job. The young people come together at a gathering; Johnny dances with Frankie and later takes her to the cinema. The episode ends with them holding hands. This sequence and those that immediately follow are told without exaggeration or sentimentality. From the beginning, however, the principal characters are seen only vaguely, and our empathy remains limited. They have no background, no family that we are allowed to see, and nothing to render them unique or memorable. One assumes that Johnny is indicative of many young men of his generation: disinherited and alienated within the confines of the cybernetic urban community. But this side of his character is ignored, and we never begin to understand—or even see—the more complex aspects of his personality.

After Johnny's first encounter with Frankie, he has a brief romantic fling with the infamous "Peaches," a young woman noted throughout the neighborhood for her lack of moral virtue:

"the first time she let you kiss her, the second time she tongued you, and the third time ———."[9] His affair with Peaches, however, does not progress, and Johnny returns to his pursuit of Frankie. Soon their friendship begins to grow. But before their relationship reaches its height, another interlude occurs, this time with Johnny and his male friends. Like many of Hemingway's heroes, Johnny must temporarily leave the city and seek the pastoral amid the company of men. On a camping trip to Lake Michigan, he walks on the beach in solitude, communes with nature, and keeps vigil all night as he contemplates his coming initiation into the adult world of love and sex. At dawn, he is ready to greet the new day: "All at once he had a notion. He let the blanket drop from his shoulders and he pulled off the loose sailor pants and jersey he was wearing. He stood up like that naked in front of the new sun. The wind whipped around his skin. He stood with his legs apart, so the air could get around him. He had never had a feeling like that before" (62). Too obvious in its use of symbolism, the passage is nevertheless effective. Johnny's identification with nature is sincere, as is his acceptance of the purification that accompanies it. The moment is rendered (unlike many other episodes in the book) in clear, concise prose; the sentences are short and declarative, and the words have a distinct effect on the reader.

Upon his return from this initiation ritual, Johnny is more sure of himself, his feelings, and his relationship with Frankie. That night, alone for the first time, he realizes that they are about to fall in love: ". . . he put his arm around her and he kissed her; it was a long tight kiss; her eyes were closed and her body was rigid; gee, she was nice; she was going to be in love with him" (78–79).

The chapter—perhaps the best conceived in the novel—concludes with the point of view switching to Frankie as she undresses alone in her room, pensively admiring her budding womanhood. She too has experienced something new and thrilling: a man has touched her body for the first time. Although their love affair will never be consummated, Levin is able to movingly reveal her fantasy of what that moment might be like:

She let her dress down, and then she felt in her own hands a funny wanting to touch the tips of her breasts. She touched them with one finger on each through her underthings, and pressed carefully, softly against them. . . . She didn't like the word virgin and she did like it. It was so sort of clear and pure. She was a virgin because she was still a girl. She had a picture of the first time the thing would happen. There was an immense white bed on a sort of a dais, and herself all in white on the bed. (89–90)

Her adolescent reverie, however, is broken by the crude singing of her older brother returning from a date:

Red-hot mamma . . .
mamma . . .
Your papa's gettin' ma-ad. (90)

The juxtaposition of her romantic female fantasy with that of her brother's male sexual ego foreshadows the conflict that will occur between Frankie and Johnny. For the moment, however, Frankie consciously or unconsciously recognizes the naive nature of her fantasy and concedes the greater reality of her brother's world: "She thought Steve knew all about women" (90).

Frankie and Johnny's romance soon settles into routine; it becomes apparent that they will neither marry nor consummate their affair, although it is never clear as to why this is so. We follow the couple to the Tivoli every Wednesday night; we learn of Johnny's daily rountine, his job, and his futile attempts to move ahead in the commercial world. But the last half of the novel, in which the failure of the relationship is linked to the failure of the American dream, is not as well conceived as the first half. Their romance dwindles, but little tension or excitement is generated by that fact. Although we understand that Frankie and Johnny are struggling to come to terms with their own sexuality,

Levin is unable or unwilling to deal directly with the sexual implications he himself introduces. Sex is not a part of Frankie and Johnny's relationship, although it is a constant source of frustration for Johnny: "He wished to Christ he could do something. She certainly wanted him all right like he wanted her. . . . He wanted to talk to her and explain the whole thing but how could you talk about a thing like that?" (134). Only in one final moment, when the relationship is irrevocably lost, can Johnny articulate his sense of frustration. In response to Frankie's habit of calling him "lover," Johnny angrily declares, "I'm not your lover. . . . I never was your lover. That's the whole damn trouble" (188).

It is obvious that Frankie and Johnny are unable to deal with the forces that dominate their lives. Yet Levin does not sufficiently explore the psychological or sociological origins of their defeat. There is no sense of tragedy in this story of fated lovers; the destiny of Frankie and Johnny remains mundane, at times even banal.

In the last pages of the novel Levin needlessly follows his two protagonists through a series of events which have little relevance to the drama that has just been enacted. The novel does not conclude with any sort of resolution or catharsis but rather with an inappropriate ironic twist. Although the affair is over, and they have gone their separate ways, Johnny continues to daydream of Frankie and even hopes to catch a glimpse of her somewhere in Chicago. But his hopes are in vain: "All the time Johnnie was thinking those things Frankie wasn't riding on the L at all. All that time, Frankie was riding home on the bus" (212).

Although *Frankie and Johnny* is too great an exposition of a limited subject matter, the novel is not without its redeeming qualities and is a marked improvement over Levin's previous effort. Unlike *Reporter*, the drama here is mostly realistic and the language is unexaggerated, neither sentimental nor hard-boiled. As Levin matured as a writer, he was able to avoid some of the flaws of *Frankie and Johnny*. He learned to be more consistent in tone, to sharpen his characterization, to achieve a more sophisticated handling of point of view, and—although not consistently—to be more aware of the requirements and restrictions of fictional form. As an early effort, *Frankie and Johnny* is, at best, an interesting and emotional work; at worst, it is uneven and vague. It also represents Levin's second and last attempt to ignore the forces that had shaped his life. In the years immediately following the publication of *Frankie and Johnny*, Levin was to rethink his desire to write from a purely American perspective. His next novel, *Yehuda* (1931), represented a new concern for the present and future security of a Jewish homeland; *The Golden Mountain* (1932) dramatized Levin's growing interest in the Jewish past.

Yehuda

After the completion of *Frankie and Johnny*, Levin decided to return to Palestine. Thus began a pattern of swinging back and forth between Israel and the United States that would continue throughout his career. He felt drawn to both cultures and saw the need for a literary link between the world's two largest Jewish communities, one that could possibly be established by a writer who understood "the perplexing relationships of nationalism, hereditary culture, [and] international idealism."[10] Levin was becoming more comfortable with the dual aspects of his identity and began to see this dichotomy as a positive manifestation of the different aspects of his personality, rather than as a debilitating conflict: "Gradually I began to feel that this utter polarization was unreal, unnecessary. If I had both elements in me, I had to give them expression, combined as they were."[11]

Nevertheless, Levin's next novel was not a reflection of this unification, but was rather an entirely Jewish book—set in a Jewish land, peopled almost exclusively with Jews. *Yehuda* (1931), written while Levin was in Palestine and based on his experiences there, is a novel about kibbutz life—the first in the English language—and represents Levin's growing belief in Zionism and peoplehood. "Here, all could be harmonized," Levin recalled. "Here in Palestine—even before the Jewish community was a nation—I could live as a Jew in a Jewish society, speaking our own tongue, raising wholly Jewish children. . . . The logic of Jewish life in Palestine was to me irrefutable."[12]

Technically, *Yehuda* represents an advancement over Levin's earlier efforts. The kibbutz, or commune, offered an ideal setting for the novel, as well as for the development of Levin's major theme. The device of the collective was also well suited for the examination of the lives and dramas of several personalities within the group. Each individual story, although connected to the whole, functions as an important variation of the central motif. Like *Reporter*, the structure, which is based on a series of interrelated incidents, is fragmentary. But unlike *Reporter*, the subject matter of *Yehuda* lends itself to episodic treatment. The series of events, characters, and situations which make up the novel are held together by the book's theme and setting. For the first time, Levin succeeded in unifying form and content.

The main theme of *Yehuda*—the clash between individual and group interests—forms the psychological center of the novel and gives unity to the book. Individual destinies differ, and conflicts are resolved in diverse ways; yet all the characters within the novel struggle to balance their individual needs with those of the collective. Although various personalities thread the narrative, the person who dominates much of the novel, and in whom the conflict is most fully realized, is the sensitive, young musician, Yehuda. Yehuda works in the kibbutz fields during the day and practices his violin at night. He dreams of going to America and playing in a symphony orchestra, a fantasy that has been actualized by a fellow musician who periodically sends him postcards from what appears to be an affluent Chicago. Yehuda's dream is not one of self-deception, for he has been told by his early teachers of his potential greatness. He is painfully aware of the struggle within himself: should he pursue his musical career or give himself over entirely to the commune and the building of a country?

Yehuda's internal strife continues throughout most of the novel. Although he enters into the daily life of the kibbutz, he remains unwilling to sacrifice his dream. The conflict is eventually resolved, at least within the context of the novel, in the final pages of the book. For years Yehuda has practiced in solitude. He has had no indication of the relative merits of his talent, no point of comparison with other violinists, no auditions, and no audience. Through a fortunate coincidence, however, Yehuda is finally presented with an opportunity to test his musical ability. A world famous violinist, while touring the Middle East, agrees to visit the settlement and give a performance on the slope of Mt. Carmel for the colonists throughout the area. It is also arranged that after the concert Yehuda will play for the virtuoso, who would then pass judgment on Yehuda's talent. If, according to the great Yussuf Brenner, Yehuda had real potential, he would leave the settlement to study the violin. When the great day arrives, however, Yehuda has an unexpected reaction to the celebrity. As a person, Yussuf Brenner is pretentious and impatient with the settlers. Somewhat of a dandy, he is disdainful of the crudity of commune life, the food, and the manners of the settlers. Yehuda is offended and refuses to play for a man who appears insensitive to the ways of his people. He declines the audition and with his refusal experiences a certain happiness and a new sense of self-confidence: " 'No,' said Yehuda. 'I play only for my comrades.' . . . Once again the great Yussuf Brenner was fitted into his duster, and in Yehuda's eyes he became a creature utterly strange. . . . Yehuda drew back among his comrades . . . and Yehuda watching him smiled a small contented smile."[13]

The novel has come full circle. Yehuda is once again seen as a farmer who plays the violin. The conflict is not permanently resolved; nor will it ever be, for such a resolution would destroy either one or the other side of Yehuda's being. His heroic stance, however, is a symbolic rejection of the postcard world of American materialism and the false pomposity of Yussuf Brenner. Yehuda has come to the realization that he belongs in Palestine and that even here, among the dust and the flies and the heat, he can play his music. The final scene is filled with earthly images of life, joy, and hope for the future: "In the hot mid-afternoon Yehuda looked out over the plain. Never before had the clean air so joyously filled his body. . . . The whole plain danced in the white afternoon heat, wavered and beat under the glow of the sun. Yehuda's eyes looked toward the field where the corn had been this year. Tomorrow he would take Maccabee's princelings and go out with Pinsker to do ploughing on that field" (373–74).

Although Yehuda's story dominates the novel—he opens and closes the book and is central to much of what happens in between—other characters complement his situation by acting out similar dramas. Mr. Paley, for example, is an American who has come to the commune for a three-month stay and is tempted to remain. Much of what Mr. Paley says represents Levin's point of view and the author's own divided loyalties. Like Mr. Paley, Levin had visited Palestine and had worked on a kibbutz for several months. Mr. Paley's attraction to the land is Levin's attraction: a sense of total cultural fulfillment and completion as a Jew living among other Jews. "In the middle of my life," Mr. Paley explains, "I have to come here and admire you fellows and know that you will be better off and happier in your life than I ever was, because you've done the right thing. That's what America does to a Jew, it doesn't give him any real satisfaction in life" (95). Mr. Paley longs to be involved with the building of a homeland, a task that would transcend his own individuality and sense of mortality: "Here you had the feeling that you were doing something, too, you were building the land of Israel, Eretz Yisroael" (164).

Although Mr. Paley has come to cherish the personal warmth and security of the commune, his ties to America and its traditions remain strong. A self-made man, he believes in the efficiency of capitalism and is often frustrated with the socialist system and the cumbersomeness of pure democracy. Although he complains of the failings of his American way of life, he cannot help boasting of its accomplishments: "Why, an American could take hold of this country and run the whole works as smooth as a factory. Why, there are single industries in America so big that all of Palestine could be run as one of their smaller departments" (96).

At the conclusion of the novel, one is uncertain if Mr. Paley will remain in Palestine or return to America. Like many of the novel's episodes, that of Mr. Paley remains inconclusive. Individual dramas have significance in the novel only in that they help convey a larger theme, one that is often repeated through several different characters.

Yehuda's and Mr. Paley's conflicts are largely internal and do not affect the fate of the entire community. The story of Sonya, a young kibbutz worker, however, takes on implications that are of consequence to the whole population. Sonya is a compulsive thief, constantly stealing small, meaningless objects. Her actions are mostly harmless and go unnoticed until it is discovered that she has stolen kibbutz chickens and sold them in exchange for silk stockings. The *chavarim* ("settlers") are outraged; a meeting is called to decide her fate, and the debate that follows continues long into the night. The issue soon takes on larger proportions than those implied by Sonya's particular misdemeanor. The men of the community are united against the women; the male principle of political and economic efficiency is pitted against the archetypal female response of protection and compassion. The men are in agreement that Sonya, as a deviant member of their society, must be expelled in order to insure the successful operation of the farm. Pragmatism must take precedence over the emotions: "This is a question in which we must set aside all personal emotions as this is a question of theory which is the very center of our code of living together as a group unit. . . . Comrades, nature is cruel, nature casts out the unfit. . . . We must send away those who are not fit to work, those who are tainted. Sonya must not be allowed to come back into the commune" (268, 270).

The women, however, are equally adament in their support of Sonya. Unlike the men, they understand that love, compassion, and brotherhood are essential to the survival of their community. Their position is more Jeffersonian than utilitarian: "We are as good socialists as you," the men are told. "But we understand that we came here first to live, to build a home for ourselves in Eretz Yisroael, and not to carry out a socialist text-book. This is a commune only as long as the commune serves the human members" (276).

Again, as in the novel's other episodes, there is no real resolution to the problem. When the meeting concludes it is decided that "Yehuda should go up to Yocheved's place and talk to Sonya, and come to a peaceful understanding"; but it is uncertain what that "understanding" will be. Unlike the stories of Mr. Paley and Yehuda, which allow for speculation, Sonya's drama is fully played out, and the choices are clearly defined. As a result, the nebulous resolution is weak and unsatisfactory.

The inconclusive ending of the "trial" of Sonya is the major flaw of the novel and serves to emphasize other, less obvious, deficiencies. Like the Sonya episode, the ending of the novel itself is tentative and inappropriate to Yehuda's character. The structure of the book is often too fragmentary, suggesting the technique of a short story rather than that of a novel. Levin's tone and language is also uneven, changing rapidly and without reason. And although the main drama of Yehuda's personal struggle remains fixed in our imagination, its power is somewhat diminished by Levin's profuse use of detail and description.

Yet Levin's sometimes inadequate handling of the material does not negate the passion and commitment to Palestine that is expressed throughout the novel. The most moving moments in *Yehuda* are those that evoke the beauty of the land and the idealism of the Zionist dream. Ultimately, individual destinies are secondary to the collective will to build a community in a new country. The members of the kibbutz, despite their idiosyncratic vanities and jealousies, never lose sight of their mission to establish a homeland where Jews can live in peace.

The publication of *Yehuda* did not occur without some difficulty. When Levin first sent the manuscript to the John Day Company in New York, his publisher reported that *Yehuda* was a "beautiful book," and that he would be glad to publish it if Levin would agree to change the ending, which he felt was not consistent with the tone of the novel. Levin interpreted this as an attempt to interfere with his artistic integrity and refused. Later, Cape and Smith Publishers decided they liked the book and accepted it without asking for revisions.

By 1931 Levin had earned some degree of recognition in the literary world, and *Yehuda* was given considerable attention by the critics. Contemporary reviews were generally enthusiastic. Lionel Trilling, writing for the *Nation* (24 June 1931), stated: "Mr. Levin has made good use of the opportunity which his material afforded him. He carefully proportions his emphasis so that the group remains whole, and yet no flavor of individuality is lost." The *New York Times* (22 March 1931) claimed that the struggle of Yehuda contained "an element of drama. And an element of poetry, too." And Leonard Ehrlich, writing for *Saturday Review* (6 June 1931), referred to *Yehuda* as "a very fine novel, eloquent and groping and pathetic as the little settlement on the rim of the wilderness."

Despite favorable reception by the critics, the book enjoyed little commercial success. Salesmen reported that the title was especially damaging. Moreover, the depression years were just beginning in the United States, and few books were selling well, certainly not those dealing with the struggles of Jewish settlers in Palestine.

The Golden Mountain

After the completion of *Yehuda*, which was written in Palestine, Levin again stopped in Paris to visit his old friend Marek

Szwarc. The two talked of religion, and Levin was fascinated by Szwarc's recitation of a number of tales about the legendary rabbis of a sect called the Chassidim—a branch of Judaism Levin knew little about. The Chassidic (or Hassidic) movement, which included in time fully one half of the Jewry of Eastern Europe, swept through the Jewish population in the eighteenth and nineteenth centuries. The sect was founded by the followers of the Baal Shem Tov (literally, "The Master of the Wondrous Name"), a miracle-working rabbi who lived in the Carpathian Mountains in the first half of the eighteenth century. Rabbi Israel, as he was originally known, taught worship through joy, song, dance, and love. His particular brand of Judaism stressed the immanence of God in all things, the sense of mystical ecstasy in the communion with God, and a joyful affirmation of life. Like many religious leaders, the Baal Shem Tov taught by word of mouth in the form of tales and parables. He wrote nothing down and was skeptical of attempts to record his teachings. After his death legends, handed down through several generations of rabbis and religious followers, preserved his teachings and testified to his miraculous deeds. Eventually these stories were written down and were circulated widely in little storybooks printed throughout Poland and Russia.[14]

Levin began reading a number of these little pamphlets which Szwarc had collected from Poland. He was immediately fascinated by what he found: "These stories sang right home to me. I discovered a whole literature of parables and miracles, of ethical fables grown out of a remote Jewish village life in the Carpathians. . . . In these tales from Poland I felt a spiritual homecoming."[15] In the Paris libraries he found a complete collection of the Yiddish storybooks edited by the Jewish Folklore Institute of Vilna. Although the philosopher Martin Buber had published early essays from his *Hasidism and The Modern Man* in German, there existed no English translation of the legends. Levin began to conceive of a book that would contain the tales of the Baal Shem Tov as well as the stories authored by his great-grandson and most famous disciple, Rabbi Nachman of Bratzlav (1772–1810).

Working from the original Yiddish, Levin began reshaping and retelling the legends in English. Whereas the stories surrounding the legend of the Baal Shem Tov had no single authorship and were simple and moving, those written by Rabbi Nachman were sophisticated and metaphorically complex. In the former, he felt a sense of personal heritage that transcended time and place. Through them he was able to rethink his own relationship to the past: "Whether there were Chassidim amongst my actual progenitors, I don't know, but through this folklore the whole Yiddish world in which my forebears had lived came alive to me with a new spiritual quality, a new dignity."[16] In the stories of Rabbi Nachman, however, Levin recognized a literary association that led directly to the symbolic literature of the twentieth century: specifically, the stories and novels of Franz Kafka. (Levin had "discovered" Kafka's *The Castle* in the summer of 1930.)

When completed, *The Golden Mountain* (1932) contained two parts. The first section consisted of twenty-six short tales, legends, and anecdotes of the Baal Shem Tov; the second contained eleven stories by Rabbi Nachman. The material dealing with the life and deeds of the Baal Shem Tov was arranged in chronological order and presented the history of the great rabbi's career. "Before He Was Born," the opening anecdote, tells the story of the Baal Shem Tov's conception—ordained by God and foretold by the prophet Elijah. Levin's translations are simple and direct, retaining as much as possible the original folk quality of the stories. "In heaven, Elijah came to God and said, 'See how the Jews suffer. It is time to send an Innocent soul down to earth to sweeten the lives of the Jews.' "[17] Several years later, according to legend, convinced that the time had arrived, "God looked over all the earth, saying, 'Where shall a man and a woman be found who are worthy of bringing into the world an uncontaminated soul, the soul of Rabbi Israel'?" (8). In subsequent episodes Levin recounted the birth of Rabbi Israel in the little city of Okup in 1700, the death of his mother after his circumcision, and only a few years after that, the death of his father. The stories trace the boyhood of the orphaned child, his joy in singing with his friends in the open fields, and his neglect of formal studies. Each tale describes another segment of his career, from custodian of the town synagogue, to a scholar of the Cabbala, to the moment when—at the age of thirty-six—the voice of God told him he must reveal himself to the world as a holy man: "Then the Master of the Name began to perform works of wonder" (44).

The tales of the Baal Shem Tov belong to folk literature. Those of his great-grandson, however, are surprisingly modern in their subtle use of symbols and images. Some thirteen stories and twenty-one short allegorical tales have been preserved from Rabbi Nachman's works; Levin recorded eleven of the most famous. His task here was somewhat more delicate than in the first half of the book, for Rabbi Nachman's narratives were filled with labyrinthine visions of the supernatural and vivid images of the mystical world of the Cabbala. Moreover, the stories were pedagogical in nature, intended to instruct readers on various aspects of religious law. Levin's rendition of these stories, while conveying their essential folk quality, also reveal a complicated pattern of archetypal imagery.

Levin was not alone to "hear the voice of [an] entire people" in the Chassidic legends. Since *The Golden Mountain* there have been many translations and interpretations of the tales, from Martin Buber to Elie Wiesel's *Souls on Fire* (1972). Jewish writers from I. L. Peretz to Isaac Bashevis Singer have made use of the rich mythology of Chassidic lore. But in 1930 Levin was among the first to grasp the significance and the beauty of the Chassidic imagination. *The Golden Mountain* remains one of the most accurate and eloquent interpretations of that imaginative spirit. Perhaps the greatest testimony of its worth came in 1975 when Penguin Books purchased the rights to *The Golden Mountain* and republished it under the title *Classic Hassidic Tales*.

If *Yehuda* represented Levin's growing interest in the present and future of Judaism, *The Golden Mountain*, which Levin referred to as his "Chassidic book," demonstrated his growing fascination with Jewish history and the legends of the past. In Palestine Levin had found a physical and social connection to his Jewish self. In the world of eighteenth- and nineteenth-century European Jews, Levin sensed a spiritual and emotional identification. Together, the two books represented a change in the direction and pattern of Levin's literary career. Although he would continue for a time to write in and of America, he would never again be consumed with the desire to repress that which was Jewish in his literary imagination.

Levin's next efforts reflect his concern for the dominant social issues of the 1930s: the economic depression, Marxist ideology, and the plight of the worker. "Proletarian" in outlook, *The New Bridge* and *Citizens* were politically motivated and—although both fine novels—limited in scope. With *The Old Bunch*, however, Levin achieved what he had envisioned for many years: a fictional rendering of the diverse forces that shaped his personality. The 1937 novel—probably his finest work—is a highly successful representation of the Jewish experience in America.

Chapter Three
The Thirties

At no time in his long and eclectic career was Meyer Levin more closely in tune with the mainstream of American fiction than in the 1930s. *The New Bridge* (1933), *Citizens* (1940), and to a lesser extent *The Old Bunch* (1937) conform to the general standards of literary tastes of the decade and reflect the social values of the nation.

It is difficult to characterize the literature of an entire literary period. One might say, however, that the writers of the 1920s, the "lost generation" of Hemingway, Fitzgerald, Pound, Eliot, Joyce, and Proust were concerned more with form than subject. The works they produced tended to be more complicated and technically polished than those of their immediate predecessors. They emphasized aesthetics, and were rarely concerned with social reform or political issues. Many of the young writers who appeared in the 1930s criticized this lack of social conscience. Rejecting most of the writers of the 1920s as "retreatists," they started out in a different direction. The writers of the depression era presumed it to be their role to help change the world and make it free from poverty. They believed in the rights of the workers and called themselves "proletarian" or "revolutionary" writers. Later, toward 1935, the term "social realists" was used to characterize such writers as Edward Dahlberg, Michael Gold, Jack Conroy, Daniel Fuchs, Robert Cantrell, James T. Farrell, and John Dos Passos. As opposed to the generation of the 1920s, they were concerned more with doctrine than form. The theory they promulgated was consistently Marxist in nature: a variation on the theme of the downfall of capitalism and the triumph of the working class. John Dos Passos, for example, possible the most typical and the most talented writer of the period (although somewhat older than his fellow proletarian writers), saw America as a land divided: the rich versus the poor. The prevailing thesis in his *U.S.A.* trilogy (1937) was that human values are destroyed by a concentration of wealth in the hands of a few.

Like so many authors and intellectuals of the 1930s, Levin was attracted to communism and the progressive ideology of the left: "From the day I sat in the Reynolds library laboring through *Das Kapital*, I had considered myself in agreement with the equalitarian aims of Marxism, and from that day on I was confronted with the conscience question before every liberal mind in our generation: if you believe in economic equality, why don't you join the communists, meaning the Communist Party? . . . I suppose that I was considered a fellow traveler."[1]

Essentially a nonpolitical writer, Levin nevertheless turned to political themes in the 1930s at least partly as a result of the prevailing literary mood. Although not radical in their ideology, *The New Bridge* and *Citizens* represent a concern for immediate social and economic realities and a point of view that is decidedly leftist. *The Old Bunch*, although more social than political, nevertheless, espouses a vaguely Marxist doctrine. Together, the three novels mark Levin's maturity as a writer and represent one of the most highly productive periods in his career.

The New Bridge

Although Walter Rideout included *The New Bridge* (1933) in his list of American radical novels,[2] the book cannot truly be called political or ideological. Yet it does, like *Citizens*, reflect the influence that the proletarian movement had on Levin during this period. Both novels have a leftist orientation and express a general dissatisfaction with the capitalist system.

The climate of social and political protest not only provided subject matter and theme for the radical novelists, but also called for a particular literary style. Throughout the 1930s there was a close connection between fiction and journalism, suggesting the influence of industrial technology on the literary arts as well as the "higher purpose" of fiction. Mostly as a result of Dos Passos's experiments in *Manhattan Transfer* (1925) and the success of his "newsreel" technique in *U.S.A.*, "higher journalism" began to have its own claim to imaginative truth. As David Madden states in *Proletarian Writers of the Thirties*: "In content, form, and intention the distinctions between journalism and fiction became blurred in the Thirties . . . writers began with the imaginative impulse and ended with higher journalism."[3] In *The New Bridge* Levin abandoned his previous experiments with journalistic techniques but maintained a realistic expository style. Much of the narration of the novel has the force of a well written news story. Events are presented in a series of juxtaposed scenes which shift back and forth between past and present action. Although individual personalities are established and developed, Levin, like Dos Passos and the social realists, was more concerned with the portrayal of environment and social systems than with the traditional problems of characterization.

The action of *The New Bridge* is confined in time to a single day. The immediate subject matter concerns the eviction of Joe Joracek and his family from their apartment and the attempts of the other tenants to band together to resist that eviction. Ironically Joracek himself has helped construct the building in which he lives. Now that the project has been completed, he is unable to find work and cannot pay his rent. As the tenants' protest progresses, a struggle with the police results in the accidental killing of Red Feingold, the fourteen-year-old son of one of the occupants. In a furious attempt to fix blame for the tragic event, the tenants "capture" one of the policemen and prepare a citizens' trial.

The first chapters of the novel show Levin's ability both as a storyteller and as a perceptive observer of human behavior. We learn that "Marks's Gardens" was conceived by its builder Simon Marks as a model contemporary tenement. Through a series of flashbacks we see the individual dramas of the various families in the building. Their personal stories are told with sympathy, yet convey a sense of impending disaster.

The cast of characters includes Joe Joracek, whose story is meant to symbolize the evils of a capitalist system that exploits and then destroys its workers. Unemployed and depressed, Joracek's self-esteem declines rapidly, as does his relationship with family and friends. Among the other tenants are Mr. and Mrs. Stratford. Mr. Stratford is an American Don Quixote who has long since lost his grasp on reality; when the police invade the building, he attacks with his World War I saber. Although his portrait is touched with humor, Mr. Stratford's story is mostly one of tragedy—a life lived in disappointment and disillusion. Next door to the Stratfords is Mrs. Feingold, the main force behind the strike. Her exaggerated and violent reaction to the entire situation becomes more understandable when one learns that her husband abandoned her many years earlier ("He walked out on me," she bitterly explains), and her life has been one of subsequent outrage and anger. Tillie Novak, a "small, frail" woman, lives on the top floor amid vacant apartments: "Tillie Novak lived on the top floor, the rest of that floor stood vacant. She felt lonely up there; lonesome most of the day alone."[4] She, like several other tenants, is reluctantly drawn into the protest and is overwhelmed by the ensuing events.

Levin's successful presentation of interesting characters and the diverse dramas surrounding them represents an unmistakable advancement in his development as a writer. Through the psychological penetration of the personalities involved, Levin was able to create a realistic, "journalistic" work that went beyond the mere reportage of events. If his attempt at creating a microcosm of a city population falls somewhat short, he does successfully convey the sense of human tragedy and the ineffectual lives of the people he portrays.

The first half of *The New Bridge*—the stories of the different families and the recounting of events leading up to the killing of Red—is forceful and convincing. After the shooting, however, the action is anticlimactic and contrived. More significantly, the focus of Levin's attention becomes vague and confused. The reader's sympathy for the worker and the plight of the poor, which Levin had earlier labored to enlist, is now lost amid the novel's other concerns. The point of view of the second half of the book, for example, shifts from that of the tenants to Simon Marks, the landlord. Instead of a greedy capitalist, Marks is presented as a pathetic man who has risen from poverty to riches only to discover the meaninglessness of his life, the alienation of his wife and children, and the loneliness of his existence. He too has been ruined by the system and is about to fall back into poverty. The last two chapters deal with Marks's existential crisis as well as with the obvious betrayal of the American myth of success. As the archetype of the self-made man, Marks's failure is seen as the failure of the capitalist system. But by this point the novel's action is too convoluted, and Levin struggles in vain to bring order to the chaotic chain of events that make up the second half of the book.

The final episode, contrived and overly symbolic, follows the two antagonists as they meet on the bridge of the novel's title—the bridge that was constructed to give access to Marks's Gardens. Joracek is on his way to kill Marks; Marks is about to commit suicide. The men recognize each other and suddenly, simultaneously, comprehend the futility of their lives. Marks shares his last few dollars with Joracek and throws away his wallet containing the symbols of his former self. The two men, reborn, go off together, presumably into some distant morning sunrise.

The unsatisfactory conclusion only serves to emphasize the novel's major weakness. Although *The New Bridge* starts out as if it were going someplace, it ends as if Levin had lost sight of his objective. As was the case in *Frankie and Johnny*, events of the second half of the novel are mostly meaningless; the narration slows down, and the action begins to lean heavily on coincidence. As a result, the novel's good qualities—effective characterization and a realistic sense of time and place—are mitigated. The reader in the end feels neither the "proletarian" thrust of the story nor the sense of personal and familiar tragedy.

The New Bridge was completed and accepted for publication in 1933 by Pat Covici, who also published Jack Conroy's *The Disinherited* that same year. Levin had high hopes that his book would be part of the new proletarian vogue: "The days of the marches on Washington and of rent strikes had come. . . . I was certain that I would be hailed as the great proletarian writer. The *New Masses* was filled with vitriolic attacks upon such ivory-tower retreatists as Thornton Wilder; a proletarian title alone, such as *Union Square*, was enough to set the logs rolling."[5]

The New Bridge, however, was not well received and did not sell well. In addition to any intrinsic problems the book might have had, it also had the misfortune of appearing on the first day of Roosevelt's bank holiday. Nevertheless, the novel represented another step forward in Levin's development as a writer, especially in terms of his presentation of character. As a sociological book that was, however, not sociology, *The New Bridge* prefigured two very fine efforts at social realism: *The Old Bunch* and *Citizens*.

The Old Bunch

Perhaps more than any other, *The Old Bunch* (1937) is, as Allen Guttmann claims, "the book for which Levin ought to be remembered."[6] A realistic treatment of the second generation of Chicago's West Side Jews, the novel was Levin's first attempt to treat the American Jew as literary subject. Prior to the composition of *The Old Bunch*, Levin's work consisted of novels that were purposely and comprehensively "American" (*Reporter, Frankie and Johnny, The New Bridge*), a book that gave literary expression to past Jewish folklore (*The Golden Mountain*), and a

Zionist novel set in Palestine (*Yehuda*). *The Old Bunch*, by contrast, is about American Jews and what it meant to be a Jew in Levin's contemporary America.

The theme of Jewish identity and the crisis of assimilation was to dominate successive generations of American Jewish writers. In 1937, however, Levin had few predecessors to show him the way. Michael Gold's *Jews Without Money* was more Marxist than Jewish. Writers like Ludwig Lewisohn, Abraham Cahan, and even the young Henry Roth were concerned with the plight of the immigrants in the new country and their cultural trauma, rather than with the difficult ambiguities and uncertainties of the first generation of Jews to be born in the United States.

Levin was, therefore, one of the first to explore the tenuous world of a generation of Jews who found themselves lost between the old world and the new. They were the children of immigrants who eagerly abandoned the traditions of their grandparents in order to assimilate, to "make it" as quickly as possible. In the process they struggled with their own identities. A few felt a deep sense of loss for an irretrievable past; others moved without remorse toward a future that ignored their roots and their traditions.

Technique. *The Old Bunch*, as the title indicates, is a group novel. Like most collectivistic fiction, concern for the individual is subordinate to concern for the group as an entity. "The bunch," rather than any single individual, is Levin's main character and the principal motivating force behind the novel's action. The group is made up of eleven boys and eight girls who went to school together and lived in the same neighborhood in Chicago. Collectively they move through the Jazz Age of the 1920s and into the depression of the early 1930s. The perspective of the narrative is always that of one of these nineteen beings. The novel has no recognizable center, no cohesive plot; each character has its own nucleus and together the loose galaxy of experience forms the pattern of the novel. Collectively the bunch forms a paradigm of American society: one becomes an artist, several are doctors and lawyers, another a professional athlete, and so forth. The movement of the novel, however, is centripetal: the center continually pulls the members of the group back. The novel's structure thus reflects the experience of the group as well as one of Levin's basic themes. Although the members of the bunch seek to enter the mainstream of American society, the peer group remains their cynosure, determining their values and standards. As Levin expained: "While novelists emphasized the individual in the family unit as the determining human relationship, I saw the surrounding group, the bunch, as perhaps even more important than the family in the formative years. Particularly in the children of immigrants, the life-values were determined largely through these group relationships."[7]

As a group novel, *The Old Bunch* has no single narrative voice. The novel is made up of multiple stories and attempts, like Dos Passos's *U.S.A.* trilogy, to encompass an entire social system. Like *U.S.A.*, *The Old Bunch* is very long; both works intend to be epics. Unlike *U.S.A.*, *The Old Bunch* is not written from an impersonal "camera eye," but from the subjective—although multiple—persona of the bunch. The point of view is that of Jewish boys and girls growing up and coming of age in Chicago. The result is a more immediate, more inescapable sense of time and place. Studying the similarities between Dos Passos and Levin, Marcus Klein notes: "With all of its devices of topicality and with all of its great efficiency in narrative, and with all its anger, *U.S.A.* does not have the sense of *The Old Bunch* that history is something that happens to *me* and to *my* friends and *my* family."[8]

Levin was influenced by Dos Passos and stated so in his autobiography. Significantly, *Three Soldiers* has a lasting impact on one of Levin's more perceptive characters. As important an influence as Dos Passos were James T. Farrell and the naturalist writers. Although Levin denied he wrote about the seamy side of life, *The Old Bunch* fulfills many other tenets of naturalism. Like Farrell (and Zola and Norris), Levin intended to describe modern society impersonally and dispassionately. Intrinsically,

The Old Bunch is, like many naturalist novels, the classic story of defeat, of the individual overwhelmed by the forces of environment and the grinding weight of a capitalistic economy. Levin's determinism however, is equivocal. His bunch does suffer the vagaries of a capricious and sometimes brutal system, but some escape, and others are only coarsened. Levin's view of man fluctuates between existential possibility and scientific determinism. Much of the novel is given over to the view that man is a victim of society, a creature responding to forces over which he has no control. But the process, Levin seems to say, is not inevitable.

Like most writers of naturalist fiction, Levin hoped to be objective, even documentary, in his approach. While writing *The Old Bunch*, he arduously researched and consulted newspaper files for background information. The bunch lives in a world that is inhabited by Big Bill Thompson, Samuel Insull, and Al Capone. Historical events, such as the Leopold-Loeb murder trial, the Lindbergh flight, the Lindbergh kidnapping, and the stock market crash are all included in the narrative.

But Levin's purpose transcended that of naturalism. The materials of Jewish life were not only important as components of realistic fiction, but essential to the novel's theme as well. In describing the world of the old bunch, Levin wanted to explore the whole complex and ambiguous relationship between ethnic and national identity. In part, the book is a personal inquiry into his own relationship to Judaism and to America. (The career of one of the characters closely follows the events of Levin's life.) Caught up in the Jazz Age revolution, the members of the old bunch, like their author, desperately seek to establish their uncertain identities in a world from which their parents and grandparents have been excluded.

Religion and Identity. One of Levin's chief purposes in depicting the conflict of generations was to demonstrate how family life and religious traditions were destroyed by the New World. The three generations of Chicago Jews represented in the novel cover a wide spectrum of religious beliefs. Totally anacronistic in the contemporary world of the bunch, is the Orthodox grandfather who brings his own dishes and food to dinner because he cannot trust his daughter's observance of the dietary laws. His generation can afford such idiosyncracies as beards, daily prayer, and Talmudic study, for they are secure in their identity and in their old-world ways. At the other extreme are the members of the bunch who seem to be in a state of flux, with no permanent, lasting values. Their standards are not determined by tradition, religion, or even family, but are purely self-generated—derived from each other and from the city about them. The parents of the bunch are somewhere in between. Immigrants for the most part, they are motivated by a drive for acceptance in what they have hesitantly accepted as their new home, rapidly abandoning a religion that seems increasingly irrelevant. Consequently they are powerless to transmit even a modicum of their faith to their children.

Traditional Judaism held little value for the upwardly mobile younger generation Levin describes. The children of immigrant Jews scrambled to partake in American history. In the process they became doctors, lawyers, artists, teachers, dry cleaners, realtors, even petty gangsters and professional athletes; but among the bunch there are neither rabbis nor Talmudic scholars. As the second generation Jews of Levin's West Side eagerly divested themselves of the encumbrances of their forefathers, genuine religion was left behind.

Instead the bunch practices a distorted and vulgar Americanized version of religious custom. At Passover, for example, Sam Eisen suggests to his wife Lil that they go to his parents' home for the traditional Seder. Her response is one of disdain: "Oh, mygod, do I have to sit like a prisoner till twelve o'clock while your grandfather mumbles the whatyacall it through his beard?"[9] Instead Lil decides to go to Ev Goldberg's, who has invited the members of the bunch, along with several Christian friends, to her own Seder. "Listen, Sam," Lil tells her husband, "We're young, we're modern. . . . Why do we have to get stuck with a bunch of old dodoes? . . . A *seder* is supposed to be a celebration, isn't it? Why not have a good time!" (384). At Ev's, canapes are served on "matt-zote" (in the presence of gentiles, the bunch is careful to anglicize all Hebrew words). A cake is brought in ("If you can't eat bread, eat cake"), topped with an effigy of Moses. The place cards are parodies of other biblical characters: "The place cards were the cleverest things! Each card was a cut-out of a biblical character, only Ev had fixed devilish little short skirts over the long gowns of the women characters, and put derby hats on the men. But the most comical thing she had done was to get pictures of movie stars and paste their faces on the biblical figures" (386). After the *Haggada* is passed around as a curiosity, the maid brings in "An immense, sugar-baked ham," which is greeted by "squeals and titters."

Not all the members of the bunch, however, are willing participants in this parody of a once meaningful ceremony. Sam Eisen, one of the novel's few idealistic characters, is disgusted and outraged. Ironically, Sam is a nonbeliever who has made an intellectual stand against religion. But he recognizes the cruel mockery of the evening, as well as his own sense of loss. At length Sam excuses himself and rushes out. Lil first thinks he is sick and then is infuriated that he would disgrace her before her friends. No one can understand why Sam, an aetheist, should be offended. Sam is unable to explain to Lil that his need for a cultural identity does not contradict his rejection of God: " 'Religion has nothing to do with it. . . . You know perfectly well, all that stuff means nothing to me. It's just the—the social side of it' " (383).

Sam had wanted to be with his parents during the holiday for himself, and because he is sensitive to the needs of the older generation: "it makes them feel good to see their son and the grandchildren at the table." But Sam is alone among the group in his understanding and compassion for his parents. For the most part, relations between the generations are marked by conflict rather than warmth, by rejection rather than acceptance.

One reason why the bunch is unable to embrace the religious traditions of their parents is that contemporary Judaism is portrayed in the novel as puerile, at times even pernicious. The rabbis that appear are contemptible caricatures; religious ceremonies are presented as meaningless parodies. A pretentious "Rabbi Dr. Joseph Rosenston, of the exclusive South Side Temple, wearing a full dress suit," for example, officiates at a wedding as gaudy and lavish as that of the Patimkins in Roth's *Goodbye Columbus.* In another episode, a young rabbi is portrayed as an opportunistic fund raiser. He appears at the University of Illinois in order to establish a "Jewish foundation" under the auspices of the B'nai B'rith. While he is there, he convinces Joe Freedman—another idealistic character—that his stand against compulsory R.O.T.C. is not really worthwhile. The rabbi is young, smooth-faced and smooth talking, and Joe reluctantly abandons his protest.

Organized religion, therefore, is not an effective pattern of self-expression for the bunch. The realization of a Jewish self, however, is at least temporarily consummated by one of the group through an identification with Zionism and the future destiny of Palestine. Joe Freedman, whose beliefs and career closely parallel those of the author, is a sculptor trained at the University of Chicago. Repeating Levin's odyssey, Freedman (the name is surely significant) travels to Paris where he meets Aaron Polansky, a sculptor who depicts biblical scenes in hammered copper. Polansky introduces Joe to the legends and history of the Chassidic Jews—just as Marek Szwarc had done for Levin. Joe is fascinated by Polansky, his work, and his retelling of the Chassidic tales. (In almost every respect, the fictional description of Joe's encounter with Polansky follows Levin's account of his visit with Szwarc.) Joe begins to understand the importance of his Jewish past as an essential part of his present self. He perceives that he is not an isolated entity, but part of a long-lasting Jewish culture. His parents, Joe now realizes, were not merely refugees, come to bear children in the land of promise and opportunity, but were also a part of this rich heritage.

After Paris Joe journeys to his grandfather's village of Kovna in Poland (as Levin had wanted to do). Here he meets a young Polish Jew who, unlike the other young men of the village, has neither the interest nor the desire to go to America: "To America? What for? What do I want to go there for? To sweat over a sewing machine? Ah, they don't fool me with their tales of diamonds in the streets. To Eretz Yisrael, that is different. There I would sweat, but I would know I am in my own land" (291). This view awakens a response in Joe and, like Levin, he eventually makes his way to Palestine and settles for a time in a commune in Safed. Here he passes several happy months, working in the fields and joining in the life of the kibbutz. But Joe, again like Levin, decides to return to America where he can pursue his career in art.

Joe is one of the few members of the bunch who is treated without scorn or satire. As spokesman for the author, he is the major thematic vehicle in the novel, linking the realistic portrayal of experience with the book's metaphysical concerns. As a sensitive artist, Joe is able to articulate the personal difficulties and uncertainties that many of the others experience but cannot expresss. His dilemma is that of his generation. Only those fully aware of the contradictory aspects of their personality, however, can begin to deal with the problems of identity and self-expression.

Theme and character. It is only natural that in addition to dealing with the themes of religion and identity, Joe utter the novel's economic "message," which is more New Deal than Marxist and certainly far short of the radical protest Levin was to espouse in *Citizens*. Although some Jewish writers in the 1930s, like Mike Gold, were members of the Communist party, most were merely leftists. Overwhelmingly they supported Roosevelt and the New Deal,[10] an attitude that is reflected in Levin's novel. Some of Joe's conclusions derive from Marx: man is alienated from his work and denied satisfaction in his career because society twists and distorts his efforts; the capitalist system frustrates even those who would work for the public good. Humanity, according to Joe, is made up mostly of the unworthy, those "mere lumps of human flesh," and the few worthy, those "who were at least aware of the stream of human life" (753). He rejects agitation for a new order, however, in favor of a slow evolutionary progress, citing Franklin Roosevelt as an example of the type of man who quietly works for change and a better society: "Every man didn't have to agitate, to be with the revolution. In every act of life, there were two ways of going, and if a man consistently, in his own life, in those decisions which confronted him, acted in harmony with the long historical wave toward revolution, why, he could claim integrity in his life. It seemed to Joe that Roosevelt was such a man and that, quietly, the American revolution was going forward" (753).

Although the novel's major themes have their greatest expression in the careers of Sam Eisen and Joe Freedman, no character is given greater attention than any other, and almost all the characters—from both the new and the old generation—help convey the acute strain of Americanization. Levin creates a variety of situations, many of seemingly minor importance, that nevertheless illustrate significant conflicts. As Marcus Klein observes: "There are few large events. The small events sometimes have a perfectly cozy smallness, but they have also the weight of the complication of cultural fact."[11] The bunch resent, for example, their original Jewish names and are quick to anglicize them: Manasheh becomes Manny; Gittel, Ethel; Shulamith, Sylvia. But when the members of the group begin to bear children of their own, they remain unsure: "Lil's folks wanted them to call the kid Jacob. . . . 'Let's humor them,' Lil said, 'Afters, we can change it to James' " (268).

There is a similar ambiguity surrounding wealth and success. Rube Moscowitz is the richest among the parents of the group, but he has profited as a result of doing business with Chicago's corrupt politicians. Rube's financial prosperity is dependent on Sam Insull, the Irish alderman who still controls the district. Rube uses his influence to further Insull's political ambitions, and Insull in turn helps assure Rube of continued commercial success.

Rube's wealth enables the Moscowitz family to master acculturation. Mrs. Moscowitz has American pretensions ("you would never see a Yiddish newspaper in her hands"); their apartment clearly characterizes their parvenu status: "The apartment was swell, too, with a full-width sunparlor and French doors. Near the gas log fireplace was a grand piano—not a baby grand. . . . There were at least a dozen lamps, floor lamps and table lamps, and Celia's mother was always buying marvelous new lamp shades at Field's" (22). In the end, however, Rube's empire collapses and he discovers too late that Insull has simply used him until it was no longer expedient to do so and then deserted him.

The eventual failure of Rube Moscowitz is symbolic of the fragility of success in the New World. Yet those of the older generation who remain faithful to the past are equally bereft. Mrs. Greenstein, another parent, is at the opposite extreme from Mrs. Moscowitz. As her name indicates, she is a "greenhorn," alienated from the manners and behavior of the members of the younger generation. When the bunch has a dance, complete with a gramaphone and Caruso records, Mrs. Greenstein rushes in to disperse the group. She is outraged and frightened when her daughter has her hair "bobbed," for she associates the latest hair-style with prostitution. Her exaggerated reaction is indicative, not only of her estrangement from the ways of her daughter, but also of the pain and frustration she has experienced while bringing up a child in a strange and confusing land: "Mrs. Greenstein's whole body was trembling. . . . Her daughter would become a whore in the streets, her daughter with the breasts that she has seen budding, and been ashamed to tell her daughter anything, . . . but how could she talk when even their languages were different, how could she tell a girl such important things when she couldn't think of the English words for them" (24).

Among the younger generation, however, there are no Mrs. Greensteins. Each member of the bunch moves toward Americanization as quickly as possible. In good Jewish tradition, they are all given excellent educations. The males move toward careers which will take them out of the ghetto and into the mainstream of

American life. In almost every case, they encounter a corrupt society in which the law of competition governs everything, including human relations. Each character is initiated into the ways of capitalism where men in business, law, and medicine are forced to live by cheating, bribery, chicanery, intimidation, and even violence.

Two of the bunch, Rudy Stone and Mitch Wilner, become doctors. Mitch, whose story is continued in *Citizens*, quickly learns the ethics of the medical profession when he discovers that it is common practice among the older doctors to operate at unfavorable odds in order to earn huge fees. Rudy's idealism is destroyed in a more brutal manner. Under the hardships of the depression, he leads a group of dissident physicians in setting up a cooperative medical clinic. The venture comes under the furious attack of the more established members of the profession. The group is expelled from the medical association and banned from the city's hospitals. When the clinic doctors discover amoebic dysentery at one of Chicago's leading hotels on the eve of the World's Fair, they naively expect the Health Department to announce a quarantine. Instead the issue is silenced, and the fair opens on schedule and despite the danger.

Three others among the group—Sam Eisen, "Runt" Plotkin, and Lou Margolis—become lawyers. Lou marries Rube Moscowitz's daughter, moves to the political right, and quickly acquires the power and advantages that come with a connection to the Moscowitz family. Runt Plotkin, on the other hand, mixes with Chicago's underworld (crime was one route out of the ghetto where prejudice placed no roadblocks). As a youth, Runt peddled fake cigars. As a law student (in a vaguely disreputable law course), he manages to avoid payment of certain fees. As a lawyer, Runt keeps his connections with the underworld. When one of the bunch's dry cleaning business is threatened with violence by the union, Runt knows where to hire a gunman to ride and protect his friend's truck.

If Lou Margolis moves to the political right, the idealistic Sam

Eisen turns to the left and embraces radical causes. In the world of law, however, as in medicine, idealism rarely prevails. When Sam brings suit on behalf of a client whom the police have beaten, it is thrown out of court. The jury, Sam later learns, was made up of the policeman's relatives. When he agrees to defend a group of Communist-led rent strikers who have been brutalized by the police, Sam finds himself confronted by a prejudiced, uneducated judge. Refusing to listen to Sam's defense, the judge shouts: "You ain't got no rights! Reds and radicals got no rights!" (647).

In addition to law and medicine, a career in sports was an equally certain symbol of acceptance. One of the group, Sol Meisel, becomes a professional bicycle racer. Noting Levin's unusual choice of activity, Allen Guttmann in *The Jewish Writer in America* remarked: "One charm of *The Old Bunch* is that the athlete is a bicycle racer rather than a boxer (as in Clifford Odets's *Golden Boy*) or a baseball player (as in Bernard Malamud's *The Natural*). Why not? Sol Meisel's races seem as appropriate as Joe Freedman's art. His scenes are, in fact, among the most memorable in the novel."[12] Sol is seen in defeat and in triumph as we follow his career throughout the course of the novel. His greatest moment comes when he wins a six-day race just as Lindbergh is completing his historic flight over the Atlantic. The two feats are cleverly juxtaposed so that Sol's victory becomes a microcosm of Lindbergh's great triumph.

The eight women in the bunch are given considerably less attention than the men. One exception is Sylvia Abramson, who stands out among the females in the group as a complex and strong individual. She is the only woman who appears to be able to bring the force of her intelligence and personality to bear upon the actions of the men around her. The others, although presented with sensitivity, are seen in a limited context; they are concerned with the prospects of marriage, families, and material success.

All the members of the bunch are finally brought together at the conclusion of the novel in a rapid succession of juxtaposed scenes. The setting is the 1932–33 World's Fair. The city seems to sparkle garishly in the night; the group is awed by an eight-story electric bulb that flashes "Chicago" across the sky. The final image of the city is a naturalistic one. The fair itself is described as "a bright scarf . . . around the neck of a consumptive"; and the city, seen from the exposition, is personified as a huge, decaying organism, its inhabitants seeking only to escape the contamination: "There below stretched the rotting lungs and the rotten guts of Chicago. Close against the bludgeon stone-head, the Loop, lay the decay of the body. North, south, and west, spread the semi-circular band of slums: frame houses, deserted blocks, buildings stripped of doors, of windows, of plumbing. It was as though the city were continually working away from the inner corruption of itself, people moving away further north, south, west, leaving a growing, festering wasteland between the new districts and the Loop" (754).

The Chicago Fair becomes the dominant image in the last section of the novel. The technique is cinematic: Levin's "camera" shifts rapidly from one scene to the next. Everybody is at the Fair as the action moves toward a final frenzied conclusion. As Guttmann notes, the suggestion is that of *Walpurgisnacht*, as the scene becomes more and more frantic in the final, apocalyptic moments:

> The huge mob that had jammed the streets of the Fair slowly contracted, congealed, until only the night-hunters, the bloody-eyed, remained. In the Black Forest, incendiary flames arose. In the Streets of Paris there was a free-for-all; tables were smashed on backs and heads, a grabbing hand ripped Estelle's gown, and the cold air met her breasts; a mob got hold of a fire hose and doused a squad of cops; . . . Runt passed through crowds, grabbed girls, got socked; . . . Lou Green was yanked awake by a cop, and found that he had passed out against the imitation log palisades of Old Fort Dearborn. (765)

As the Fair closes, Mitch Wilner goes home to his wife; Runt Plotkin picks up a new girl; Mort Abramson "whizzed down Sheridan Road at sixty-five in the new airflow DeSoto"; and Harry Perlin, at home, unable to sleep, listens to the cowboy tune that ends the novel: "Git along, little dogie, git along, git along" (766).

The final refrain seems to indicate that the members of the bunch will continue to survive as best they can in an imperfect world. As Guttmann observed: "There is no reason to believe that Chicago's 'Century of Progress' has brought the millenium, but there is good reason to think that the old bunch will continue to get along."[13] This view is supported by Levin's own assertion that he "wrote with the object of revealing a whole organism, much of it repulsive, parts of it in decay, but within which there remained a great capacity for self-renewal."[14] The novel, however, does not concentrate in any positive way on individual development or fulfillment. The capitalistic system thwarts and frustrates even those with the best intentions. One or two among the bunch rebel, but most are beaten, bewildered, or lost. Despite Levin's contention, one is left more with a feeling of despair than of hope for individual or societal renewal; and there seems to be an ultimate prophecy in the way the drunken mob wildly tears the "Century of Progress" to pieces.

Conclusion. Levin had written *The Old Bunch* on an advance contract from Reynal and Hitchcock, the first time he had been able to make such arrangements. There were objections, however, to the book's heavy emphasis on Jewish characterizations, and the book was rejected in spite of advance payments. "To turn down a book after making an advance on it," Levin recalled, "was simply to say that it was hopeless."[15] Fortunately this was not the case, for the book was subsequently accepted and published by Viking Press. Hoping for greater sales, the company de-emphasized the novel's Jewish subject matter in their advance publicity. Nevertheless—perhaps because of its ethnic orientation, perhaps because of its length—*The Old Bunch* had limited commercial success. The book was criticized on the one hand by such popular magazines as *Time* because it was "too self-consciously Jewish." On the other hand it was condemned by organized Jewish groups and rabbis for its "negative" view of Jews and Judaism.

Despite the novel's initial commercial failure, critical reception was warm and abundant. The *Saturday Review* featured a picture of Levin on the cover of its 13 March 1937 edition along with a lengthy review by James T. Farrell. For the most part Farrell was laudatory, calling *The Old Bunch* "one of the most ambitious novels yet attempted by any fiction writer of his generation, a work which demands discipline and intelligence that are as yet unmatched by most novelists of his age." Harold Strauss, who was to remain an enthusiastic admirer of Levin throughout this period, wrote in the *New York Times Book Review* (14 March 1937) that *The Old Bunch* was "a landmark in the development of the realistic novel," and that it "brilliantly succeeds in taking the reader on a memorable tour of the world in which the old bunch lived." Literary critics of the day all seemed to have something to say about the novel, both pro and con. Alfred Kazin, writing for *Books* (14 March 1937) called Levin "a novelist without spectacular talent," but referred to the novel as "astonishingly well sustained." Philip Rahv, in the 3 April 1937 edition of *Nation*, praised Levin's "ambitious efforts," and "fidelity of social observation," but found the novel to be lacking in tension and "somewhat monotonous." Harry T. Moore, in *The New Republic* (7 April 1937), was similarly equivocal, criticizing Levin's ability to establish believable characters and the lack of psychological depth within the novel, but concluded that "on the whole it is a very fine novel, with the speed and lustiness and brawling of the world's fourth largest city."

Despite the novel's generally fine qualities, it was not, as most critics observed, without defects. Like most collective novels, *The Old Bunch*, as Moore noted, provides little psychological understanding of characters. The group novel was particularly useful for Levin's depiction of the milieu of the bunch and for his portrayal of the differing social manners of three generations of Jews in America. The creation of highly individualized characters, however, is subordinate to the realistic representation of environment and social patterns. Characterization tends to emphasize the general rather than the specific: characters in the novel are differentiated more by the ideas they represent than any particular idiosyncracies they may have. The process of acculturation is seen as a social phenomenon; in only a very few cases is Levin interested in the interior life of an individual whose idea of self is undergoing change and development.

Levin's great achievement in *The Old Bunch* was his accuracy of detail, his successful recreation of a specific time and place. But like most realistic fiction, the novel sometimes relies on documentation rather than on drama. As a result, situations and characters at times become gratuitous, without meaning or aesthetic relationship to sustain them as art.

But perhaps the novel's greatest flaws are simple ones, problems that seem to diminish much of Levin's work. *The Old Bunch*, like the earlier *The New Bridge*, and the later *Citizens*, is totally lacking in humor. Although Levin did write one comic novel much later in his career (*Gore and Igor*, 1969), he otherwise remained a totally serious writer. *The Old Bunch* is written with complete sincerity, and perhaps it is the fault of Levin's good intentions that accounts for the solemnity of tone throughout.

More significantly, the sheer bulk of Levin's one-thousand-page statement takes away from the power and force of the novel. Throughout his career, Levin demonstrated a proclivity for the gigantic. *The Settlers* (1972) is a lengthy (832 pages) epic of the history of Israel; its sequel *The Harvest* (1978) is hardly less voluminous—650 pages. *Citizens* (1940), like so many of Levin's works, loses tension and drama as a result of a too lengthy discourse on a limited event. Interestingly, *The Old Bunch* was a much longer novel in the original manuscript and only at the request of his publisher did Levin agree to shorten it somewhat.

None of this, however, is ultimately fatal to the novel. Despite its shortcomings, *The Old Bunch* succeeds as art because of Levin's considerable ability in several areas. He is writing of people and places he knows. The reader is allowed to participate in the history of the bunch (indeed it is impossible not to), and it is is this sense of immediacy that gives the novel its lasting significance. Moreover, Levin demonstrates a mastery of language in *The Old Bunch* that goes far beyond the patronizing attempts at vernacular in *Reporter* and *Frankie and Johnny.* The novel is written in sharp, effective colloquial prose, a technique he perfected in the intervening years in the newsroom. His use of dialogue, Yiddish intonation, and the jargon of the young is accurate and appropriate to character and situation. Levin employs language as an important indicator in the process of acculturation. One comes to know the place of each character on the sliding scale of Americanization through his manner of speech, from the Yiddish expressions of the older generation to the Jazz Age slang of their children.

The most distinguishing aspect of the novel, that which sets it above Levin's other works and gives it prominence among novels of self and society, is its integration of form and subject matter. *The Old Bunch* is constructed carefully; its structure—individual narratives revolving around the collective consciousness of the group—reflects the historical pattern of experience Levin wishes to convey. The form of the novel allows for the intersection of cultural history and the individual. To be sure, the structural tension that makes it possible to explore the tenuous relationship of the two is not maintained throughout. There are times when Levin yields to the type of social history that minimizes the role of the self. But generally, the novel maintains a balance between the depiction of society and that of the individual, between social history on the one hand and poetry on the other.

Unquestionably, *The Old Bunch*, in 1937, was Levin's most enterprising and best conceived project. In retrospect, it is probably the finest achievement of his career—a work in which an important theme is treated with sensitivity and understanding. He was one of the very first to explore the themes of assimilation, acculturation, and the crisis of identity. *The Old Bunch* remains a seminal work in American Jewish fiction. Unfortunately, although Levin continued to write about Jewish characters and themes, he never returned to the fundamental issue of Jewish identity in America. Perhaps he thought he had exhausted the subject; perhaps, too, many other authors began in the 1950s and 1960s to address similar problems; perhaps other issues, such as the war and the tragic events of the holocaust, became more important to him after 1940. Levin's next book, *Citizens*, is a fine proletarian novel. But the sense of personal involvement, the feeling that one is reading personal history, was never again captured. In many respects, *The Old Bunch* marked the zenith of his career, and Levin was correct when he labeled *The Old Bunc*h his "*magnum opus.*"

Citizens

The Old Bunch was a product of personal experience, one that was both painful and dramatic. As Alfred Kazin remarked of Jewish writing produced during this time: "There are experiences so extreme that, after living them, one can do nothing with them *but* put them into words. . . . This was already the case with many of the young Jewish writers just out of the city ghettos, who began to emerge in significant numbers only in the early 30s."[16] As the decade drew to a close, however, so did the literary careers of many of these same young Jewish authors. Frustrated on the one hand by the failure of their political hopes, and on the other hand by the inability of their books to sell, most found themselves intellectually or emotionally adrift. Levin, now the author of five novels—none of which had had even a modicum of success—also began to feel his will to continue in the literary world slipping. Nevertheless, and despite the affliction of what he came to refer to as "the monster," or writer's block, Levin produced one more novel of social realism before he came to ignore, almost entirely, the sociopolitical situation in America.

Technique. *Citizens* (1940) is Levin's fictionalized version of the events surrounding and leading up to the 1938 Memorial Day Massacre which occurred during the "Little Steel" strike in Chicago. On that day Levin himself witnessed the clash between police and strikers which left ten workers killed and seventy-five others injured. Levin's involvement with the labor movement had originated with his membership in a group called "New America," made up of what he termed "non-communist progressives": "I joined, then, a group called New America, whose history is typical of a score of organizations that attracted non-communist progressives at this period. . . . They believed that the Communist Party should not be attacked, but that nevertheless the truly progressive movement in America would have to come through indigenous channels."[17] New America took an active role in union activities and helped organize the 1937 steel workers strike, as well as the subsequent protest against the slaying of the ten workers. As a member of New America and a strike "sympathizer," Levin was present at both the Memorial Day events and the later La Follette congressional hearings into the killings. He observed everything with the eye of a journalist and with the intention of one day presenting it as a documentary novel: "I felt from the beginning that I would one day write a novel about this strike, and I watched and took part in the struggle so that I might be able to present the whole view of a strike as a social phenomenon."[18] It was not until several years later, after an intervening trip to Spain and then Palestine, that Levin was able to begin work on his strike novel.

Levin approached his material as a social realist. He began to familiarize himself with the work of the men he wanted to portray. He tried to determine what the exact relationship of a routine laborer was to his task, whether he felt a sense of productivity, of self-worth in his work. Like any efficient journalist, Levin began to observe firsthand the huge steel mills in and around Chicago. He received permission to "study" the mills and spent months drifting around in overalls. In order to be close to his source, Levin rented a hotel room in Gary, near the mills. He took his meals in a nearby boardinghouse frequented by the steel workers. Mornings would be spent at the mill, afternoons writing, evenings in taverns or union headquarters. Gradually workers came to accept and talk with him. They began to tell him what he hoped to learn, not only the economic facts of their lives, but their inner world as well: their dreams, their fears, and their hopes. He began to understand the meaning of the workers' lives, their relationship to the economic system, and their role in the class struggle he saw taking place in America. He started to visualize his novel, not only as a realistic document of a strike, but also a narrative of the lives of individual workers: "I began to see my story as built around a series of life-accounts of the workers. I would imagine the lives of the ten strikers who had been killed. I would place each of these men in his own operation, follow his work in the mill, and between their life stories I would thread the narrative of the strike, so that each portion of the novel furthered the other."[19]

Levin's use of the "interpolated life story" (as he termed it) resembled that employed by Dos Passos in *U.S.A.*, which also contained a number of biographical "sketches," or life stories, interwoven into the narrative. Levin, like Dos Passos, wished to explore the relationship of the individual to society and to the economic structure of the country. In *Citizens*, Levin interrupts the narrative nine times in order to tell the individual stories of the slain strikers. In this way he was able to juxtapose the drama of the strike with the more personal life histories of the individuals involved. Although the events of the strike are true—and much of the congressional hearings are taken verbatim from the records of the La Follette Committee—Levin's biographies are fictional, invented to suit his purpose and represent the working class. Through this combination of actual events and psychological invention, Levin hoped not only to reproduce reality faithfully but also to explain the inner forces that helped to create those events.

Characters. The novel's main character is Mitch Wilner, the young doctor of *The Old Bunch.* (*Citizens* was originally planned as part of a series of novels based on characters from *The Old Bunch.*) Through Wilner's narrative consciousness, Levin unifies his story and gives it ethical force. More or less by accident, Wilner witnesses the massacre that takes place during the course of the strike. As a doctor, he is called on to help and quickly becomes professionally, intellectually, and emotionally involved in the strike. He becomes the doctor of many of those injured and subsequently becomes intimately connected with the whole complex series of events that follows. As a result of his dismay at what he discovers, he becomes politically "radicalized" and is at once Levin's political pupil and spokesman. The novel is the story of Wilner's quest, his search for explanations, and his attempt to accurately determine culpability. As a laboratory scientist who has left his medical experiments to enter the wider (and more pernicious) world of politics, he seeks to understand the nature and origin of the class struggle. The story is told in the third person, but the point of view is that of Wilner: what he learns, the reader learns. Wilner enters into dozens of discussions of politics, economics, and the labor movement in an effort to understand the American class struggle and its inherent violence.

Unfortunately, the character of Mitch Wilner is not fully or intricately developed. Although he has many long discussions, his contribution is mostly minimal as he is tutored by others in leftist theory. Levin's objective in inventing the character of Wilner was not so much to create a complex personality as to use him as a vehicle to advocate a certain viewpoint. Without a definite identity, Wilner exists more as the author's mouthpiece than as a memorable personality.

The dramatization of the strike, the subsequent activities of the citizens' protest committee, and the senatorial hearings in Washington form the basic unity of the novel. Nevertheless, only 100 or so of the novel's 650 pages deal with the strike and its outcome directly. The rest explore the lives of the people surrounding and involved in the event. The actual events of the strike are interrupted in order to present the lives of nine of the ten men killed. (The story of the tenth casualty, Stanley Dombroski, is traced by Wilner himself.) Although fictional, there is much attention to realistic detail, as Levin tried to create a composite of actual lives of the mill workers. Not all the portraits are successful; some are too obviously stock representations, others are too flat and never come to life. Several others, however, are both convincing and moving.

The portrait of Ladislas Wyznowski ("Wyzy"), for instance, is a simple yet convincing portrayal of a hard working laborer. Like many of the other strike participants (and those killed), Wyzy is not a committed union activist. He is attracted to the march by curiosity and a childlike sense of holiday spirit. En route he refers to the demonstration as a "parade" and a "picnic," and he is disappointed to discover that there will be no music. Wyzy is described as a "good" man, a family man with two big daughters for whom he would like to find husbands. He is basically a farmer, not a union worker. And it is his love of farming and growing things that ironically causes his death: "When they came up near the police lines and spread off the road, he spied a patch of garden someone had planted in the prairie. Radish spears and carrots were coming up. 'Look this! Hey, don't walk on this! Here is garden!' Wyzy buzzed around the patch like a wing-flapping hen, chasing the marchers away from the tiny seeded area. 'Here is garden.' "[20] Moments later Wyzy is killed.

The next portrait, that of Oscar Lindstrom, like Wyzy's, is intended to evoke sympathy and support for the workers. Here too, the account of Oscar's plight is moving because of Levin's convincing journalistic technique. Oscar's son, Gus, is killed on the day of the strike, and he himself is blinded as a result of his injuries. Oscar is able to transcend his tragic experience, however, and becomes both a symbol and an eloquent spokesman for all who had suffered and died on Memorial Day. His speech at the Committee hearings, one which is placed among actual testimony taken by Levin from the La Follette records, is one of the most skillfully handled passages in the book.

Almost all the victims are immigrants: their names are obviously ethnic and their speech is distinctly non-American. In giving us this "cross-section," Levin often relies on hyperbolic language for effect. But it is also a sincere effort (one that was rarely attempted in the 1930s) to dramatize the plight of Mexican-Americans, black Americans, and the various ethnic groups that inhabited the mill towns of the Midwest. Jesus Hernandez ("Mex"), for example, is a Mexican who has come to the United States in search of a better life. His English is minimal, and he does not really understand the purpose or the nature of the strike. His life has been one of continual disappointment, poverty, and disease; his violent death during the demonstration is seen merely as the logical conclusion of a meaningless life.

The story of Ephraim Law, the only black killed during the strike, on the other hand, is filled with curious irony and an unusual understanding of the ambiguous situation of the black man in America. Ephraim's life is carefully traced, from his career in the army to his involvement in the labor union. He is a proud man, and his life history has been one of acceptance in the white man's world. As a soldier in France, he was courted by white women; as a worker in the steel mills, he had "a job as good as many a white man." The tragic irony of his life, however, becomes apparent only at the moment of his death. Wounded and losing blood rapidly, he is denied emergency treatment at a white hospital and dies as a result: "When the police picked the wounded strikers off the field, they loaded Ephraim into a wagon with other wounded, and that wagon stopped at a hospital, and some of the worst wounded were lifted out, but when it came his turn, he heard them say: 'Uh-uh. Better take the jig somewhere else.' They kept him in the wagon and drove a long time. He knew he was getting weaker. But that hospital was not a place where a man like him could go in" (629–30).

Although Levin makes little attempt to justify the actions of the police (and although the portraits of the dead men are carefully drawn to enlist the reader's sympathy for the worker), he does make an effort to understand those things that lead to violence, that set man against man. The police are not treated simplistically, nor are they seen as the incarnation of evil. Levin examines the individual personalities of three Chicago policemen present at the massacre and discovers that one, Gorcey (the "bull cop"), is by nature a man of violence. The others, however, appear to be victims of circumstance. Captain Wiley has been led to believe—and naively accepts—that the strike as well as the nation's problems can all be blamed on the communists. Ernest Braden, the most typical of the three, is not a particularly violent man, nor does he radically differ in his beliefs and life-style from the strikers. He has, however, been deliberately whipped into a state of fear and hatred by his superiors. Guilt, then, becomes collective; and evil, as the conclusion of the novel indicates, is both impossible to localize and perpetual.

Theme. All the characterizations, including that of Mitch Wilner, help convey the sense of tragedy and horror that prevailed during the 1937 strike. But in describing those events and their implications, Levin aimed at transcendence. The clash between workers and police is intended as an objective correlative for the social malaise that afflicts American society. The novel, however, seems to circumvent important issues, and the social theory that is promulgated is neither extremely radical nor very leftist. As in *The New Bridge*, members of the working class are seen as victims; but the source of evil, the novel implies, cannot be eliminated. Although the law of competition seems to corrupt all that comes under its crushing weight, the book is also hostile to communism, describing the party's philosophy as inimical to individual freedom: "they kind of distrust the mass of men; they meet in their own caucuses and figure out how to move the men one way or another" (565). Moreover, Wilner's radical education is never fully realized. At the novel's conclusion he is not politically committed, nor has he found suitable answers for the questions he continually asks.

Levin seems to be philosophically stranded midway between capitalism and communism. Despite the good intentions of Wilner and his fellow travelers, the system is shown to be larger than any individual and resistant to efforts of change. Levin's alternative, the only one the book offers, is a rather vague doctrine of existential free will. The future of progressive society depends, not on any particular political or economic system, but on the vigorous exercise of individual responsibility. Toward the end of the novel, the blind Oscar Lindstrom—who is nevertheless a man of "vision" —voices this theme: "The way I see it," he explains to Wilner, "no other system of government is going to give us any more democracy so long as we ourselves don't use it. A communist government could go in tomorrow, but if the whole population wasn't active in it all the time, it would still be a few of the people running the rest of the people" (568). Unfortunately, the novel offers no portrayal of the interior life of a responsible individual who struggles with free choice, and Levin's view of society in *Citizens*—as in *The Old Bunch*—is one in which men are seen as victims rather than as existential heroes.

Conclusion. *Citizens*, like *The New Bridge*, is a novel of social protest. Artistically, it is superior to *The New Bridge.* One tends to overlook Levin's shortcomings in *Citizens* because of his generally successful portrayal of human suffering and social conflict. The language is mostly reportorial, which suited Levin's intention of "using only actual, attested events as materials."[21] Levin sees detail with a journalistic eye and records events as a spectator. The novel is a vivid depiction of the workers' struggle against overwhelming odds. More significantly, it is a successful attempt to understand the wider forces that motivate man toward strife.

Like both *The New Bridge* and *The Old Bunch, Citizens* is a variation of the collectivistic novel. Individual characters and characterizations are important only as they relate to the wider context of American society. Unlike *The Old Bunch, Citizens* reflects the author's preoccupation with class struggle and leftist doctrine. As a result, the creation of individual personalities is sacrificed to the portrayal of social history. Like so many writers of the left, Levin presented "typical" situations in order to dramatize the plight of the worker and the poor. The pitfalls of such a technique for the novel are obvious: the emphasis on the general is inimical to at least one of the demands of fiction—the creation of complex, idiosyncratic characters. The portrayal of "mass man" was seen by Levin not as a literary liability, but as the logical extension of certain political principles: "It should be remarked that the group novel itself, developing in our time in contrast to the novel of the individual, is a reflection of the progress of equalitarian ideas, of democracy, of the sense of the interrelationship of human beings reaching ever greater importance."[22] But Levin failed to grasp the wider implications of this philosophy: man's alienation from his fellowman and the difficulty inherent in human relations. Although in many ways *Citizens* is a forceful novel of social protest, it tends to ignore the crucial area of personality and character development. Unlike *The Old Bunch, Citizens* does not maintain the balance between a presentation of societal problems on the one hand and the individual on the other. As Chester E. Eisinger observed: "Even for Levin's own purposes of protest and reform, the relationship between the self and society is impossible, freezing the individual into immobility as it does. In a larger sense he has simply failed to find a suitable structure that will present self and society together."[23]

After *Citizens*, Levin planned to continue in the genre of social realism. Other characters in *The Old Bunch* were to become the focus of future novels. The events of World War II, however, and the traumatic discovery of the Nazi holocaust were to have an enormous effect on Levin. After the war his writing became distinctly Jewish in theme and subject, and eventually Zionistic in its outlook. *Citizens*, then, was a culmination of Levin's proletarian interests which began with *The New Bridge.* The three collectivistic novels that he produced in a seven-year period constituted a considerable advancement over his earlier efforts; in many cases they surpassed the literary quality of his later work as well.

In 1940 Levin, already the author of seven books, had still produced nothing but commercial nonsellers. Nor was he an anomaly among his contemporaries: the aborted careers of many of the promising young American Jewish writers of the 1930s seemed to proclaim the general demise of Jewish writing in America. It wasn't until a decade later, with the emergence of such authors as Saul Bellow and Bernard Malamud that American Jewish literature began to mature and flourish. Levin, however, was not to be a part of this renaissance, for he had already turned away from the inner world of the American Jew and the concomitant themes of assimilation and identity. With the exception of his best-selling *Compulsion*, Levin's fictional preoccupation for the next three decades would be with world Jewry—the implications of the holocaust and the promise of the Zionist dream. Curiously, throughout this period, no other American author chose to deal with these subjects. For good or bad, Levin's literary school after 1940 was to be his own.

Chapter Four
Search for Identity

After *Citizens* was completed, Levin visited the war zones of Spain as a correspondent. Unlike many of his contemporaries who joined the Abraham Lincoln Brigade and fought against Franco, Levin did not stay long and remained out of immediate battle, a fact which prompted him to reproachfully remark several years later: "It seems to me that I am still apologizing a little for not having remained to fight in Spain."[1] Consequently, after the actual publication of *Citizens* in 1940, Levin was eager to lend his support to the latest war effort. In 1941 he joined the Office of War Information as a writer-director-producer of documentary films. Later, he was assigned to the Psychological Warfare Division and worked in London and Paris. But in 1944, after being dismissed for attaching himself without authorization to the forward troops, he became a war correspondent for the Overseas News Agency and the Jewish Telegraphic Agency, with the special mission of uncovering the fate of Jewish survivors of the concentration camps. In this role he began to discover the horrible facts behind the rumors of genocide and mass incarceration. He was horrified yet obsessed with his task. Robert Gary, a fellow correspondent, recalled that Levin "was known in the press camps for his Jew mania, riding in his jeep sometimes ahead of the tanks that first entered the concentration camps. Dropping every other role as a writer, he returned to the reporter's basic job of simply getting people's names. From camp to camp Levin rushed in his jeep, gathering lists of survivors, until months later a social agency took over the job."[2] This direct and very personal confrontation with the reality of the holocaust was to have a decisive effect on Levin's future thought and writing. The war gave him new purpose and direction and resulted in a total absorption, as a writer and as an activist, in the fate of Jews everywhere.

As soon as the war ended, Levin went to Palestine, then in the midst of its own struggle against the British. In 1947 he completed the filming of *My Father's House* (also published as a novel later that year), the allegorical story of a young concentration camp survivor who searches for his family in Palestine. He then traveled to Europe, became active in the Haganah underground (the illegal immigration of Jews to Palestine), and succeeded in filming and producing *The Illegals*, a startling view of the underground exodus of a group of Polish Jews across Europe and into Palestine. Although the film did not have major international repercussions as Levin had hoped, *The Illegals* remains one of the only authentic documents of the smuggling of Jews into Israel. Together *The Illegals* and *My Father's House* represent Levin's renewed desire to dramatize the plight of the diaspora Jew.

My Father's House

From Levin's experience with the survivors of Hitler's concentration camps came the need to express the ineffable horror of the holocaust and its aftermath. In *My Father's House* (1947) and several other works which followed, Levin attempted to fictionalize an experience and a period of history that exhausted the powers of understanding. *My Father's House* is concerned not only with the tragedy of those who perished but also with the emotional destruction of those who survived. Set in Palestine, it is also the story of the settlement of a new land and of the regeneration of the Jewish spirit. Aesthetically the novel seeks to establish a tension between the nightmarish experience of the past and the image of hope for the future in a Jewish homeland. The story intends to be both political in its Zionist setting and psychological in its analysis of the rehabilitation process.

My Father's House takes place in Palestine in the years following the war in Europe, just prior to nationhood. As in *Yehuda*, there is an appealing (and somewhat romantic) picture of settlement life. Levin's pioneers are courageous and optimistic; the land is filled with beauty and sunshine. Within this idyllic setting, the novel also aims at presenting the particular psychological problems involved in reconstructing the lives of those who suffered the atrocities of Fascism, the struggle of the refugees to regain some degree of dignity, normality, and happiness.

My Father's House, which was based on the screenplay of the same name thereby reversing the usual process, has as its central character a young boy of eleven. The novel opens as the boy, David Halevi, and his fellow refugees arrive secretly at the port of Haifa: "Now the man in the prow of the small boat flung his rope, and a hundred hands caught at it, but David was sure it came directly to him, and he was the first to seize hold of it. He pulled, and they all pulled, and the small boat rubbed alongside of the *Hannah Szenesch*. They saw other boats coming directly behind it. A voice whispered up to them, '*Shalom Yehudim*! Peace Jews!' "[3]

David, we subsequently learn, is from Cracow. When Nazis with machine guns began herding Jews into the city's main square, David, at his father's urging, fled. He is told to run into the woods, and that "after everything was over" he would find them again "in Palestine." Remembering his father's last words, David is determined to survive and to reach the land of Israel. For two years he lives in the woods—stealing potatoes at night, hiding by day—until the Nazis catch him and take him first to Auschwitz, then to Buchenwald. When the Americans arrive several years later to liberate the camp, David is still alive and still obsessed with his father's promise. Along with other liberated prisoners he joins the Haganah and begins the long, clandestine journey to Palestine, always recalling the words of his father. When the ship carrying human contraband finally arrives at Haifa, he is certain he is about to be reunited with his family and thinks only of this reunion that must be imminent.

Once in Palestine, David is placed in a children's refugee colony but remains alone and withdrawn: "He could have no friends. . . . He would be alone in the world until he found his own people. Then everybody would know, then everybody would see that they had been wrong. He would come with his father and mother to this place" (107). At the first opportunity, he runs away from the colony to seek his family. He is found, however, before he travels far and is placed in a special home for orphans. But David (now changed to Daavid) refuses the knowledge that he is an orphan like other orphans and again flees. This time he succeeds in reaching Tel Aviv, where he finds a violinist in the symphony named Halevi. Disappointed that the man is no relation, David is nevertheless encouraged by word of another Halevi—a worker in the potash plants by the Dead Sea. The compassionate laborer, touched by David's story and his apparent misery, pretends to be his uncle. For a time David lives with Yehuda Halevi, his wife, and their newborn baby. Inevitably, David discovers that Yehuda is not his uncle and sets out once again to find his true family.

David eventually reaches Jerusalem where he learns of a registry of survivors from Europe. Entering the ancient city, he becomes lost in its narrow mazes and dark streets. Alone, frightened, and exhausted, David begins to lose his grasp on reality. Priests encounter the lost boy on the Via Dolorosa and lead him back to an ancient synagogue in the Jewish section. Here, amid bearded patriarchs and Hassidic children, in a state of near delirium David repeats his constant question: "Is this the place where I can find the names of the fathers?" And an old Jew responds: "The names of the fathers? Here we have the names in the Torah, of Abraham, Isaac, and Jacob, Seth, Noah, and all of our fathers' fathers" (157). Helpless, lost, increasingly disoriented, David is joined by a group of children dressed in Purim costumes with beards and long robes, chanting and singing. In David's mind there is a confusion of images: he can no longer distinguish the children from their elders, the costumes of the past from those of the present. The last remnant of reality is dissolved for the young boy as the children around him begin to chant a Purim song, itself an eerie reminder of another, more ancient holocaust: "Haman, Haman, hanging high, / He said all the Jews should die" (162).

It is at this point that David stumbles into the Registry of Missing Persons, where the names of the war dead as well as the survivors are kept. The place itself is tomblike, as if containing the remains of the dead themselves: "At the end of a long dim hallway a large arrow, painted on the wall, pointed to an arched stairway that led down, down, as into a dungeon. . . . Daavid came into a narrow vaulted room. On the walls were long sheets of paper, printed lists of names, and people were standing in front of the lists, running their fingers down the long columns" (163–64). It is here that the boy learns that his entire family is truly dead. As he emerges from the registry, dazed and bewildered, the crowd of Purim children with their incongruous beards again surround him. Weak and insensate, David collapses into unconsciousness. He is taken to the Hadassah Hospital in Jerusalem where his slow rehabilitation and symbolic rebirth begin.

Throughout David's odyssey Levin describes the inner world of a young boy who has suffered the trauma of war and separation and who steadfastly sticks to the only illusion that could give his life meaning. But David's search has a dreamlike quality, which gives the novel much of its charm and meaning. The link between David's mental disintegration and the story of Purim, for example, serves to unite the image of past Jewish history with that of the present. The parallel between Hitler and his Persian counterpart, King Haman, further extends Levin's motif of the timelessness of Jewish suffering. Talking of the novel, Levin claimed that he intended David's ordeal to be "the external unending ordeal of every Jew, where the present becomes fused with the past through parallel and repetition, and time ceases to exist, and all history is forever present, living within the soul of every Jew."[4]

Although David's story is central to Levin's theme, there are gathered around David Jewish refugees from throughout Europe. Each helps illustrate Levin's theme of the holocaust and the difficult process of rehabilitation. Weisbrod, for instance, is an emotionally broken, brilliant surgeon who slowly emerges from his trauma to find a measure of fulfillment in the farm work of a kibbutz. More important to the novel's theme is Marta (transformed to Miriam), who more than any other character represents the psychological and spiritual wounds inflicted by the Nazis. She is drawn to David by her need for a child and because of her desperate search for love. Her past, however, has left her emotionally broken, and she cannot give herself fully to that relationship or any other. Before the war she had been the wife of a Viennese teacher. Later, at Auschwitz, her husband and child were sent to the crematorium while she was spared to be used as a prostitute. Her degradation at the hands of the Nazis and her subsequent self-imposed guilt have been so great that she can feel neither joy nor love. As her friend Avram (one who believes in new beginnings) says of her: "She would be among those who hurt themselves in their perversity, deny themselves what they most wanted out of some obscure need to continue suffering" (60). She is a negativist and a fatalist; to her David's search for his family is an illusion that must be destroyed, as her suffering has shattered all sense of possibility for her.

Miriam, however, is mostly alone in her absolutism and in her pessimism. The pioneers that David encounters are impatient with finalities, for they know that new life can be created out of faith and impossible dreams. "In our little country," he is told by a waiter in a café, "everybody finds what he seeks" (95). And throughout Palestine David discovers settlers who have rejected the horror of the past in favor of a sense of hope and new beginnings. The Jews David meets are universally kind, brotherly, and optimistic. With the exception of the British military, everyone is good to him, including several Arabs who play benevolent roles in at least two important sequences. Throughout the novel Levin projects a utopian image of a land where a sense of true community prevails. The kibbutz, with its communal kitchen, dining room, children's house, and town meetings, is seen as an ideal synthesis of cultural and productive activity.

Taken literally, Levin's view of Palestine and the Jews who have arrived to claim the land of their fathers is too joyful, too idealistic, and too enthusiastic to approach reality. Taken metaphorically, however, the image of Palestine just before independence becomes a symbol of rebirth and hope for a future that will eventually overcome the dark image of death and destruction that has followed European Jews for centuries. Seen as such, the novel projects a poetic and lyrical view of a transcendent people and a timeless land. The motif of regeneration is seen in the land as well as its people: images of the sun and the sea abound, as do the fruits and vegetables that have grown from the once arid desert. David encounters babies, children singing, and settlers who shout: "*Am Yisroel Chai*! The nation Israel lives!" From the moment David's group of tired European refugees wade ashore, they are seen not as lost survivors but as part of the renewal process: "They came in a bunch, their soaked, broken shoes gathering mud in the light soil. Zev noticed that they were mostly short, stunted, the survivors, but no longer starved looking; many had become sturdy. And among the young women he noticed a few who were pregnant" (18–19).

The two opposing motifs of the novel, that of the birth of a nation versus the memory of the death camps, is resolved through the successful rehabilitation of David. Levin's mythic tone and his biblical references throughout imply the universal nature of David's quest. The story of a small boy looking for his father becomes that of the archetypal wandering Jew searching for sanctity and a homeland. Eventually David finds refuge, for he is able to accept the land of Israel as his physical and spiritual home. The settlers teach him to find happiness in the living achievements of the homeland. His search for his biological father is abandoned, for he has come to accept the paternal security of the ancient promised land.

My Father's House, unlike many of Levin's other works, is limited in size and scope. It is a simple story, warmly told and set amid the beauty of a biblical and timeless land. But although the novel is set in Palestine and has as its subject the settlement of that land, it intends to be a psychological study of the holocaust survivors as well. In choosing to deal with such a theme, Levin set an impossible task for himself. The details of David's breakdown, for instance, are obvious, but we are allowed little insight into the details of his recovery. His rehabilitation comes suddenly, without explanation, relying heavily on coincidence and symbolic suggestion. Released from the hospital, David watches as the land for a new settlement is cleared. As the work progresses, David's friends uncover the ruins of an ancient building, the stones of which are inscribed: "Avram picked the earth out of the graven lines, and the letters of the inscription became clear. It was a curious and awesome thing to find, for they were the letters of the name of an ancient Hebrew house—Halevi" (191). All present, of course, are overwhelmed by the "miracle" that has just taken place, and the novel concludes with David's acceptance of this sign as a symbol that he has truly arrived at his "father's house," the house of Israel: " 'We'll build our house on this stone,' Avram said. 'The house of Halevi,' Miriam said to Daavid. Daavid put his hands on the stone. 'The house of my father, Yisroel' " (192).

Miriam, too, ultimately experiences an unexpected change of attitude. After resisting all efforts in her direction of friendship and warmth, she is suddenly taught to believe in the beauty of life and love. In one of the final scenes, she is seen dancing with the settlers who sing, "Joy! / . . . Yes we must / Learn joy!" (187). Levin suggests that her union with the euphoric pioneers will be permanent and that her story ends happily. Her rehabilitation, however, like that of David, is not supported within the story and therefore remains unconvincing. Although Levin aims at a realistic understanding of the inner worlds of David and Miriam, he relies too heavily on myth, allegory, and symbol. Moreover, set in Palestine, with its emphasis on the birth of a national homeland, the novel's conclusion diminishes the horror of the holocaust, and the reader tends to forget the past, as do Levin's survivors.

My Father's House is therefore only partially successful in expressing the terrifying aspects of Hitler's concentration camps. Levin deals with the experience indirectly, through the memory of the survivors and the dreamlike world of David Halevi. But if the novel does not fully succeed in rendering the dreadful reality of the past, it is nevertheless successful in its presentation of an image of hope for the future. Levin's renascent Jews are idealized, but their behavior seems inevitable when placed against the dark background of central Europe. There is a sense throughout *My Father's House* of a people who have suffered, who have had their dignity taken from them along with their homes and their families, and who have now come to a place that is historically their own. They have, by the very fact of their survival, learned to dream grandly, to sing in their work, and to reach out to each other in love. Levin has captured these settlers, not in the realistic milieu of their mundane tasks or the petty arguments that are a part of communal living, but rather in the very first burst of enthusiasm and optimism that must have been present in the early days of nationhood. Levin's emphasis on the future is intended to affirm his belief in the worth of the human spirit in the face of the inhuman. *My Father's House* presents an image of the ancient land of Palestine as living proof of the strength of the Jewish spirit and of a people who have refused to perish.

The Illegals

In the summer of 1947 *My Father's House* was concluded: both book and film were ready. The novel was published in the United States by Viking Press, and the film received its first showing in Palestine. The project had taken two years to complete; Levin had sold half of the small parcel of land he had earlier purchased in Palestine in order to help finance the production. The results seemed worthwhile: "People who had no particular sentiment toward Palestine," Levin recalled, "were intrigued by the film, while people with a background of emotion for the subject were deeply moved, sometimes overwhelmed. As a first production effort in Palestine it was far from a failure, if only for the remarkable translation of the country into film, if only for the faces of the people."[5]

Levin was still haunted, however, by the thought of another project, a film he had intended to make before *My Father's House*. Two years had gone by since the end of the war and still Jews were not permitted to emigrate to Palestine. Survivors were creeping over the borders of Poland and Hungary; illegal ships were crossing the Mediterranean and being halted and turned back—sometimes with violence—by the British. Levin recognized the tragic implications of what was taking place and felt that he could help sway world opinion by recording the story of this urgent yet illegal exodus: "It seemed to me that under our very noses, in our own time, there was an exodus as difficult and stirring as the first exodus was from Egypt. How could it be left unrecorded? . . . For me, inwardly, this would round out a self-imposed task, it would somehow complete my war job."[6]

Levin went to Europe and worked for a time with the Haganah, the Jewish underground. Through them he began to make contact with several Jewish organizations, urging them to arrange for him to film the illegal operation. Eventually they agreed to sponsor the project and put forth $25,000 to cover expenses, with Levin volunteering his own services. The actual filming took longer than expected—almost a year. At one point, Levin interrupted his work to make a short, twenty-minute documentary entitled *Voyage of the Unafraid*, which recorded the seizure of a ship carrying illegal immigrants. The longer film, which traced the entire escape route, was finally completed in June 1948. *The Illegals* documented a complete underground operation, from the cities and towns of Poland, across the guarded border lines, into the crowded holds of a freighter, to the waters of Palestine where, within sight of the promised land, the ship was seized by the British Navy. All the events of the film actually took place; there were no actors and nothing was staged. Recording was done en route, involving considerable risk for Levin and his small crew. The film itself had to be hidden from the British and smuggled off the captured ship.

Although Levin was satisfied with the finished project, *The Illegals* did not have the impact on world opinion he had hoped it would. Distribution problems plagued the film, and it was shown only sporadically in New York, Paris, and Palestine. Difficulties with the sponsoring organizations ensued, and Levin's hope for a wide audience began to dwindle. Yet the film was an important landmark for him, a public and private memorial to the hardship and tragedy endured by those who tried in vain to reach the sanctity of Palestine. In one sense, the project touched Levin personally, for it brought him back to Poland, the country he referred to as "the source-land of European Jewry." Many years earlier he had declined the opportunity to visit the homeland of his parents, but now he felt that such a journey was part of a growing awareness of his own sense of Jewishness: "I had to go there, to touch Poland before I was free. Perhaps, too, I had to re-enact for myself the exodus. Then my own journey would be rounded and complete."[7]

In the years immediately following *The Illegals*, Levin began to work along more personal lines, to define his experiences in terms of his own identity, and to explore more intimately his role as a Jew and as an American. The result, published in 1950, was an autobiography, fittingly entitled *In Search.*

In Search

Levin's fictional work has always reflected personal experiences and preoccupations. *Reporter* was written at a time when Levin worked in the newsroom; *Frankie and Johnny* was based on an episode in Levin's own life; *The Old Bunch* had its genesis in personal experience, as did *Citizens.* In talking of *My Father's House*, Levin revealed the deeply personal aspect of David Halevi's search: "I knew that what I expressed in the film, the father-search, was not only the child's story, and the story of all the survivors, but my own story. Vaguely, I knew that I was terribly haunted by the story of the little boy and his strange relationship to being a Jew. . . . I had resolved all this through a device, through rebirth and the finding of a stone that perhaps could never have been there. Was my own stone there? Was my own stone to be found?"[8]

Throughout his career Levin struggled with the task of defining his ambiguous relationship to two cultures. *The Old Bunch* portrayed Jewish characters and their attempts to fight their way out of the ghetto and into the mainstream of American life. But although Levin drew on real experiences and people, *The Old Bunch* remains a work of fiction, a creative work that adheres to the demands of its genre. Autobiography, by contrast, offered Levin an opportunity for a more direct means of self-evaluation and a more subjective, if less dramatic, exposition of the Jewish psyche. *In Search*, like *The Old Bunch*, describes the interplay between society and the individual between character and environment. Levin's objective in the former, however, is more personal, one that aims at self-understanding rather than an understanding of society in general.

Many American Jewish authors have turned to autobiography in an effort to understand the Jewish experience, a task that must by necessity take into account the peculiar relationship of American Jews to both their religion and their country. Ludwig Lewisohn Mary Antin, Anzia Yezierska, and more recently, Alfred Kazin and Herbert Gold, have all sought in autobiography a means of defining their own special images as Jews living in America. For Levin the problem was further complicated by the fact that he not only felt a basic conflict within American society, but also a strong identification with the state of Israel: "I had since early manhood been passionately involved in the development of a Jewish civilization in Palestine. Twenty years ago this had seemed a strange absorption for an American Jew, but now it appeared that I had not been on the wrong track. But some of the old questions took a new turn. What was my relationship to Israel? to America? to the world? More insistently than ever I had to ask myself, What am I? and What am I doing here?" (3–4).

For Levin the American Jewish experience was difficult to describe; the social, intellectual, political, and economic freedom that Jews had achieved by mid-century only served to complicate the story. In contemporary America, Levin wondered, was the Jew clearly definable, immediately recognizable? In earlier societies—Germany, Poland, or Spain, for example—the Jewish personality stood out in sharp relief. Although the Polish Jew or the Spanish Jew was influenced by his environment, the essentials of his Jewish life and character were distinctly preserved. As Jay David observed in *Growing Up Jewish*: "In the Old Country a man was a Jew first and *then* a Russian, Frenchman, German, or whatever. In America he was first and foremost an American. The European ghetto assured rabbinical leadership in both secular and religious affairs; the American rabbi simply could not control a congregation scattered for miles around."[9] Levin's "search" therefore was for a basis of understanding, not only of his own identity, but on a larger scale, of how a Jew functions within a majority culture that is not historically his own.

The basic dichotomy of Levin's existence and the central issue of the book is stated early. "Was I an American, or a Jew?" Levin asks, "Could one be both?" *In Search* is, as Levin asserts at the outset, "a book about being a Jew." It is a long work—over five hundred pages; the tone is mostly confessional, and the mood is one of self-examination. The events of the past, both political and personal, are recounted from the vantage point of the present and interpreted through Levin's acute sense of Jewishness. Levin is a novelist who has roots in America, in the Jewish traditions of the past, and in Israel. In almost every episode he attempts to assess each of these factors in order to develop some kind of personal equilibrium.

The book is divided into three parts, each representing one aspect of the synthesis of his personality: Europe, America, and Israel. The headings also reflect Levin's physical movement, his journey from Chicago to his old-world roots in Eastern Europe, and then to Israel and an acceptance of a new, bicultural identity. Levin's odyssey back to Poland and then forward to a Zionist future in Israel metaphorically suggests the author's subjective movement toward self-discovery. Levin's journey is circular in nature, leading him out of isolation and back into the community of man. He must return to Vilna, the place of his parents' birth, to understand his own identity as a Jew, before he can move toward the future and comprehend the full meaning of peoplehood and the land of Israel: "I had to touch Poland before I was free. . . . Then my own journey would be rounded and complete" (369–70).

Part 1, "America: The Self-Accused," begins with Levin's early memories of life in Chicago where social tensions between hostile minorities brought him to a premature sense of alienation: "My dominant childhood memory is of fear and shame at being a Jew" (5). One learns of Levin's boyhood on the West Side of Chicago, his editorship of the high school newspaper, his literary group at the University of Chicago, and his first writing apprenticeship with the *Chicago Daily News* where he was able to rub elbows with some of Chicago's finest writers: Ben Hecht, Maxwell Bodenheim, and the young John Gunther. His early efforts at fiction are described: short stories published (almost ashamedly) in "Jewish" journals and his first "American" novels, *Reporter* and *Frankie and Johnny.* Part 1 also tells of Levin's early association with Zionism, his first trip to Palestine, and his stay on a collective farm near Haifa (the experience of which formed the basis of *Yehuda*).

In addition to the recounting of personal experiences, *In Search* is a firsthand report of much of the literary and political history of three decades. The events of the 1937 Memorial Day Massacre, for instance, are told in great detail and without the fictional clutter of *Citizens.* But more often there is an eye toward self-discovery and toward discerning the more personal meaning of world events. We follow, for example, Levin's short-lived experience with the Spanish Civil War, his growing apprehension over the threat of Fascism in Europe, and the events leading up to World War II. Part 1 concludes on the eve of the war, with Levin's premonition of the horror that was about to take place.

Part 2, "Europe: The Witnesses," is dominated by the story of the Nazi holocaust and Levin's own discovery of the tragic fate of six million European Jews. Although the shortest of the three sections, it is in many ways the heart of the book. Levin's melancholy yet obsessive odyssey through Hitler's crematoria understandably became one of the most significant experiences in his life and helped solidify his commitment to the future of world Jewry. Perceptively, Levin acknowledges the impossibility of expressing the unfathomable atrocities of Nazi Germany: "From the beginning I realized I would never be able to write the story of the Jews of Europe. The tragic epic cannot be written by a stranger to the experience, for the survivors have an augmented view which we cannot attain; they lived so long so close with death that on a moral plane they are like people who have acquired the hearing of a whole range of tones outside normal human hearing" (173).

Instead Levin gives a moving account of what he discovered as he traveled through the sites of Hitler's death camps and of his own strained emotions as he learned of the millions dead and the living dead who emerged. "I am sick of telling their stories," Levin writes of the survivors, "for there is no issue from their dreary tales. . . . It isn't a fourth of the Bulgarian Jews and a fifth of the Polish Jews and a third of the French who survived; they all have death inside" (175). Above all else, it was the survivors and the wreckage of their lives that touched Levin: "Each who found himself spared by what seemed to be a succession of miracles was haunted forever by the unanswerable Why. Why I? What must I do to pay for this that I was spared? What made me leave the house on an errand just before the Gestapo arrived? Why was I unhurt when I jumped from the train, while the others were shot by the guard? Surely this was a sign that I was spared for something" (177). All this transcends memoir to become history that is at once personal and universal. As Max Lerner observed of *In Search*: "Levin has a swift, economical and unpretentious style, but he also has the inner eye which relates the outer event to the psychic demands of a devouring heart."[10] It is to these demands that Levin addresses himself in part 2 and discovers his link, not only with the dead of Auschwitz and Dachau, but also with the whole of the Jewish past and its future.

In part 3, "Israel: The Released," Levin attempts to specify the implications of this connection with history and his relationship to the new nation of Israel. This last section recounts the filming of *The Illegals*, the documentary about the Jewish underground to Palestine. The clandestine flight of the Jewish survivors and Levin's involvement with the "Bricha," as it was called, is told in great detail. We learn of the difficulties and dangers that were part of the filming of the exodus, the multitude of heroic and tragic episodes experienced by the voyagers, the seizure of the ship by the British while Levin covertly filmed the encounter, and the subterfuge by which the film was hidden from the British military. The style and method is that of a good reporter. But again Levin's purpose is ultimately personal, as he describes his own "psychic demands," his sense of responsibility to the European survivors, and his urgent need to be a part of the future of Israel.

The book closes with some philosophical reflections on the relationship between Israel and America, and with a call for mutual understanding and support between the world's two largest Jewish communities. Having his roots in both, Levin naturally wants to build a bridge between them. For his part, his "search" is concluded in Israel where his earlier doubts have been replaced by a renewed commitment to Judaism. The central dichotomy of his life—his Jewish and his American identity—is resolved through an ultimate acceptance of the positive aspects of biculturalism: "I do not . . . feel that I am an issueless dilemma as an American and as a Jew, and that I must renounce one culture or the other. I recognize that some individuals may feel, and for themselves rightly feel, that they have to do this. But we also know that there can be successful bicultural and multi-cultural personalities, and I do not see why the modern Jew shouldn't strive for such a realization, if it gives the best expression to all that is in him" (536). Furthermore, Levin concludes, Jewish civilization will continue to flourish because of a living Israel, a land which will stand as a metaphor for the survival of the Jewish people as well as for universal justice: "The example of Jewish history in the past few years can give courage to all humanity: if there was a messianism in the Jewish folk that enabled it to rise out of death to attain Israel, then humanity as a whole must possess the fuller messianism, and contain within itself the force to attain peace and justice" (547).

Despite these somewhat meaningful observations, *In Search* suffers certain philosophical weaknesses. Specifically, Levin's need to somehow see a purpose to the chaotic events of the first half of the twentieth century is unrealistic. Israel did indeed rise out of the horror of the holocaust, but Levin searches in vain for a cause and effect relationship. As with so many Jews who lived through the age of Hitler (and surely Levin's involvement was personal and traumatic), Levin had to live with the knowledge of enormous atrocities and somehow try to justify the ways of God to man. His explanations, however, appear pointless and necessarily contrived, thereby diminishing much of the validity of his conclusions.

More significantly, Levin's claim that he had resolved his particular identity problem and had embraced the Jewish aspects of his personality does not negate the assimilationist, self-doubting tone of the rest of the book. Levin is troubled throughout by a feeling of guilt, of inferiority, and by his inability to "make it" in a gentile world. Levin's early "fear and shame at being a Jew" is hardly mitigated as an adult. "For all my labors in the last years to fit myself into the world pattern," Levin tells us, "I was still a little member of my clan, over-anxious, self-centered, insecure, the eternal bright and troublesome Jew. As soon as I got into the world among the Goyim, I messed up" (171).

For the most part, however, *In Search* is rewarding. Like all good autobiography, the book maintains a balance between individual awareness and historical truth, between self and the world. Although large sections of *In Search* are devoted to Levin's personal grievances, which could have been omitted, the book remains a sincere effort at self-evaluation. As such, it provides a personal form of psychoanalysis as well as a momentary catharsis: the telling of the story imposes order upon it. Without the need to universalize experience, Levin has told the story of what being a Jew means to him. At the same time, it is a perceptive treatment of the generic problem of assimilation and the inherent conflicts of Americanization. The strength of *In Search* ultimately lies not in the philosophical observations Levin offers, nor in any solutions he presumes to find, but in the sincerity and the urgency of the quest itself.

The manuscript for *In Search*, which was completed in 1948, was refused by almost all the major publishing houses, possibly because of Levin's frank criticism of the publishing industry, or possibly because the publishers feared libel suits by some of the people Levin had handled rather roughly. Frustrated, suspecting some sort of collusion against him, Levin finally had the book published in 1950 in Paris at his own expense: "A crazy, impractical thing, I knew. Conceited, too—trying to put myself among the Paris-published geniuses, the Joyces and Henry Millers. Still, printing was cheap in France, and I had to get the book off my mind."[11]

He sent copies to several illustrious personalities, including Thomas Mann and Albert Einstein, and received some encouraging responses that he was eventually able to use as jacket quotations. Thomas Mann wrote that *In Search* was "a human document of high order, written by a witness of our fantastic epoch whose gaze remained both clear and steady. . . . It will serve those to come as a source of enlightenment and as a living image of all that we had to experience." Levin was equally buoyed by the response of Albert Einstein, himself a Jew, who stated: "In this book, the Jewish problem and fate has been grasped in all its depth. The author's wisdom is derived not from what others have written, but from his own chain of experience and observation, forged through the artist's creative fire, and tempered by his extraordinary aptitude for observation, his psychological insight, and his striving for honesty and truth."[12] Although encouraged, Levin was still without a publisher and without any means of distribution. The book remained entirely unknown, and Levin was left with virtually the entire edition.

Finally an offer for publication came from a small, relatively new house called Horizon Press and after that, an offer from a British publisher. Gradually the book was accorded mild critical support and enjoyed a moderate commercial success. Some years later, after *Compulsion* (1956) had made the name of Meyer Levin better known, and while American Jewish literature in general was enjoying a great popularity, Paperback Library brought out another edition. In 1973, after the book had been out of print for over a decade (the same year as the publication of his second autobiographical work, *The Obsession*), Pocket Books, a division of Simon and Schuster, published a paperback edition of *In Search* for mass distribution.

The Diary of a Young Girl and *The Obsession*

Soon after the Horizon Press edition of *In Search*, Levin came upon Anne Frank's *The Diary of a Young Girl*, just published in France from the original Dutch. The book had received warm reviews in Europe without, however, attracting a wide readership. *The Diary*, a young Jewish girl's beautiful and moving story of how she and her family lived for almost a year in fear and hiding from the Nazis, immediately overwhelmed Levin. He began a campaign to have *The Diary* published in English and made into a play. And thus, unwittingly, Levin began what was to be an agonizing, prolonged struggle that was to bring years of bitterness, courtroom battles, and enervating confrontations with some of the leading figures of the literary and theatrical world. The controversy, which occupied much of Levin's time and energy for almost two decades, is fully recounted in *The Obsession* (1973), Levin's second autobiographical work.

When *The Diary* finally appeared in English, Levin's front-page review in the *New York Times Book Review* helped launch its extraordinary career. From the beginning, Levin had been the foremost advocate of *The Diary*. He had established a warm relationship with Otto Frank, Anne's father and the sole survivor of the Frank family, and had served as his unofficial representative and "agent" in the United States. For this, he received no fees, but it was understood that Levin would dramatize *The Diary* for stage production. He interested Cheryl Crawford, a well-known Broadway producer, in the project, and it was agreed that Levin would write the adaptation. His first draft was accepted and an abridged radio version, which was aired on the *Eternal Light* program, was widely acclaimed. But soon afterward Miss Crawford called Levin and told him that, upon consultation with her friend Lillian Hellman, she had decided the play was "unstageworthy." The material was handed over instead to Albert and Frances Hackett, and it was their version that was eventually produced on Broadway by Kermit Bloomgarden.

The Hacketts' play proved almost identical to Levin's version; he decided to bring suit against the Hacketts and Bloomgarden for "appropriation of ideas." The case went to court, and a trial jury ruled that the Hacketts had indeed followed the basic pattern and many details of Levin's original version. Levin was to receive one half of the royalties the Hacketts had earned from the dramatization. In other words, the jury expressed the opinion that Levin's version had contributed as much as the work of the Hacketts to the success of the play.

Despite his courtroom victory, Levin's play remained suppressed by the owners of the dramatic rights. Subsequent attempts in Israel and the United States to have the play produced have not been allowed. A student production of the original play at Brandeis University was stopped by court order. Similary, a production by the Soldiers' Theatre in Tel Aviv was forced to close after only fifty performances despite the fact that it received excellent reviews and was generally judged to be superior to the Broadway version.[13] Other attempts to have the "illegal" play produced have met with similar legal barriers. In the August–September 1976 issue of *Midstream*, Benno Weiser Varon, a former Ambassador of Israel and scholar of Jewish affairs, tried to piece together the many strands of this strange story and concluded as follows:

> Frank's lawyers refused even to allow amateur productions of the Levin version. . . . Whatever the legalistic aspects of this basically moral question, Levin's never-ending efforts to see "his child" come to life deserve understanding and sympathy. And he got such—in petitions signed, i.e. by Albert Camus, Norman Mailer, Isaac Bashevis Singer, and scores of other writers. After all, the Hacketts have experienced the gratification of world-wide performances, have won a Pulitzer Prize, other honors, and money galore for a drama that the jury found to be largely derived from Levin's work. There exist three major plays on Jeanne d'Arc. Why not two on Anne Frank? The answer is, of course: to avoid comparisons.[14]

Levin's successful litigation established that the Hacketts had followed the structure and outline of his play. But Levin had not proved another far more important point, one that was to be at the heart of his "obsession" for the next twenty years: there was another reason for pretending that his version was "unactable." According to Levin, Hellman and her crowd objected to the play, not because it was dramatically inappropriate, but because it was "too Jewish." Upon close examination of the two versions, one finds that the Hacketts' play had indeed been subtly dejudaized: certain passages were omitted and others manufactured in an attempt to make the play more universal, more ecumenical, and thus more accessible to a wide audience. Specifically, the Hacketts eliminated one of the most touching passages of *The Diary*, Anne's passionate reference to the inability of escaping one's Jewishness and her proud acceptance of that fact: "Who has made us Jews different from all other people? Who has allowed us to suffer so terribly up to now? . . . We can never become just Netherlanders, or just English, or representatives of any other country for that matter, we will always remain Jews, but we want to, too."[15] At one point in the drama, however, the Hacketts did write into the script something that was never uttered by Anne, either in her diary or in Levin's version: "We're not the only people that've had to suffer. There've always been people that've had to . . . sometimes one race . . . sometimes another."[16] One other outstanding change also occurred: the Hacketts totally omitted any mention of the Franks' hope for survival in a Jewish homeland. Although references to Zionism appear in the first pages of *The Diary*, and although Anne's sister Margot (who was to die in Bergen Belsen) talks of becoming a nurse in Palestine, there is no mention of the subject in the play.

Levin believed the suppression of his own version, with its specific references to Jewish identity and Zionism, was an extension of the type of attacks on ethnic expression he had experienced throughout his career. In spite of his court victory, he became emotionally involved, "obsessed" as it were, with proving the authenticity of his claims. What followed was a long financially and emotionally consuming struggle. Petitions were circulated; a full page advertisement was placed in the *New York Times*; Levin received the reputation of being litigious, disputatious, even paranoid. For his part, Levin remained acrimonious. He began to see the suppression of his play as a personal vendetta against him, one that had application in other areas as well. All this is told, twenty years after the incident, in *The Obsession* with great bitterness: "With a kind of passionate vindictiveness my enemies have not only made incredible efforts to keep this work suppressed, but have extended their animosity, so that I have since the trial come to feel my whole career as a writer slowly eroding under unremitting denigrating campaigns, whispering campaigns, and sometimes through plain blacklisting" (202). *The Obsession* is full of examples of what Levin considers to be victimization by a cabal against him: television interviews canceled for no apparent reason, talk show appearances refused, even a newspaper interview with his wife mysteriously withdrawn when it was discovered that she was married to Meyer Levin "the author."

Although there is probably some truth to his claim that a "literary mafia" had conspired against him as well as other writers, Levin was never able to prove fully his allegations. The writing of *The Obsession,* however, allowed him to exorcise the anger that had consumed him for so many years. The emotional strain, to be sure, had been costly. But even during the height of *The Diary* incident, Levin was able to write effectively, for in 1956 he managed to produce one of his most memorable works, the best-selling *Compulsion.*

Compulsion

During Levin's early years as a student at the University of Chicago, he had worked as a part-time reporter for the *Chicago Daily News.* But when Ben Hecht moved to New York in the summer of 1924, Levin became the star feature reporter. He was somewhat apprehensive about the job he had stepped into at the young age of eighteen and remembered feeling "like the inheritor of an oversized mantle." His work, however, consisted largely of "two-minute railway station interviews with movie stars who were passing through Chicago; . . . [and] detailed descriptions of gangster funerals."[17] Then came the Leopold-Loeb case, the most talked about event of its time. All of Chicago was bewildered yet fascinated by the nature of the crime and the strange motivation of the two precocious university students who had killed for "intellectual" reasons. As Levin recalled: "From the day of the finding of the mutilated body of the little boy Franks, this crime fascinated the world, and little else occupied our minds in Chicago. It seemed to us that we were in the center of the world through its purest crime—a crime, as we thought, for crime's sake. It was an intellectual crime, committed by two brilliant university boys in, it seemed to us, an almost abstract experiment in immorality."[18] The reporters in the newsroom of the *News* felt themselves to be especially involved in this "intellectual" crime, for the case was broken by two of the *News'* reporters who were able to match the ransom note to the typewriter that connected the two boys to the murder. (Mulroy and Goldstein, the two reporters, later received a Pulitzer for their work on the case.)

When the trial hearings began, Levin was sent to write features. He felt close to the case, for in a curious way he identified with with the criminals. The pair were the same age as Levin and, like him, they were students at the University of Chicago. He had not known them personally, for they, like their victim, were members of extremely wealthy south-side Jewish families, whereas Levin was from the much poorer West Side. Yet as a young intellectual Jew, Levin felt that he understood them, their alienation from their parents, their pathological intellectual curiosities, and their obsessive need for experience: "In a confused and awed way, and in the momentary fashionableness of 'lust for experience,' I felt that I understood them, that I, particularly, being a young intellectual Jew, had a kinship with them. . . . Their act was an extreme expression of an unwholesomeness perhaps due to our being strangers to our parents and our past, unsure of our place in society."[19]

The story, with its many psychological and moral implications, stayed with Levin for many years. But it was not until the onset of the Anne Frank affair that he returned to the material. Pressed by financial concerns and upset by the emotional drain of the incident, Levin turned to his publisher for suggestions and was reminded that some of his best work had emanated from his own Chicago experiences. Perhaps he had other Chicago themes to explore? Levin recalled the Leopold-Loeb case, a subject that he had for years carried in the back of his mind. His publisher's initial reaction was a positive one, and Levin began to conceive of a documentary novel that would nevertheless explore the psychological ramifications of the murder and the personalities involved.

Several aspects of the crime particularly interested Levin. First, it was one of the earliest cases in which a psychoanalytical study of the defendants had been attempted. The defense presented its case from the psychological point of view. With the aid of testimony from psychiatrists, the boys' past and present were probed in an effort to determine their mental condition. The aged yet still brilliant and dramatic attorney for the defense, Clarence Darrow, pleaded that this type of investigation was valid in a court of law and that the criminal must be studied with the same thoroughness as the crime.

The latent philosophical implications of the crime also captivated Levin. Both Leopold and Loeb were readers of Nietzsche, Cabell, Schopenhauer; they believed themselves to be Nietzschean "supermen," above the mundane legal and moral laws of society. In retrospect Levin began to see the similarity between their twisted application of Nietzschean doctrine and that invoked by the Nazis in Germany not too many years later. He was also struck by the obvious comparison between the Leopold-Loeb act and the murder in *Crime and Punishment.* Although Raskolnikov's crime possessed an economic rationale, he too believed himself to be "superior" and above common social laws. A student and an intellectual, he sanctioned his crime—as did Leopold and Loeb—through his philosophy. As Levin later observed: "The Chicago killing was rather a step toward abstraction in the philosophy of self-made law. For in this case economic and social justification was absent. Only the idea of self-license, of superiority to common social laws, was retained."[20]

There was a third, perhaps somewhat less identifiable, factor that led Levin into the story as well. Leopold and Loeb were both sons of wealthy German Jews, a group that had always maintained a certain superiority and sense of exclusivity in dealing with the more recently arrived and poorer Russian and Eastern European Jews. Levin recalled that there was an undercurrent "almost of vengeful satisfaction" on the part of Chicago's Russian and Eastern European Jews that these were the sons of German Jews. Here then was an opportunity for Levin, the son of Russian immigrants, to vicariously match his wits against these intellectual killers from Chicago's wealthy Jewish community: "Least of all the themes eventually to be noticed in *Compulsion*," Levin explained, "was the sensitivity of the reporter-detective as a Jew of Russian extraction, pitted against the pair of thrill-killers with their superman philosophy."[21]

Despite this undercurrent of divisiveness, Jews throughout the country were mostly united in their sensitivity to the possible anti-Semitic reaction that the case might create. Jewish communities expressed a mood close to relief that the victim too had been Jewish. Although the racial issue was never overtly raised in the case (being perhaps eclipsed by the more sensational suggestion of sexual perversion), Jews everywhere were painfully aware of the fact that the murderers were Jewish.

All of these phenomena concerned Levin, and ultimately his novel reflected the many psychological, sociological, and philosophical implications of the crime. *Compulsion* did more than document the sensational murder and subsequent dramatic trial; it also explored the complicated ramifications of these events and their effect on the collective conscience of a nation. *Compulsion* became an instant best-seller. Correctly or not, the novel remains the work for which Levin is remembered.

Technique. The idea of a documentary novel appealed to Levin. His fiction had always been close to fact, and his most successful works have almost always been those that have emanated from historical events. He proceeded, as he did in the writing of *Citizens* (his other "documentary" novel), by first researching the actual accounts of the event—in this case many of his own newspaper reports of the kidnapping and murder. He followed this with interviews of families and friends of both the victim and the killers, and then spent many hours with Nathan Leopold in his prison cell. (Dick Loeb had been murdered in prison several years earlier, supposedly the result of a homosexual disagreement.)

The facts of the case were well-known: in 1924 Richard Loeb and Nathan Leopold, Jr., as an intellectual exercise, devised the "perfect crime." The murder was staged as a kidnapping for ransom, but the boys meticulously planned to kill their victim, collect the ransom before the body was discovered, and use the money for a pleasure trip. Part 1, "The Crime of Our Century," recreates the events leading up to the trial; part 2, "The Trial of the Century," encompasses the actual report of the trial itself. The first section, which incorporates much of what Levin discovered in the psychiatric reports of the case, utilizes a series of kaleidoscopic flashbacks in order to explore the inner thoughts and motivations of the killers. The story is narrated by Sid Silver, a precocious young reporter and Levin's fictional counterpart, in a style that reflects his journalistic precision: "I was lucky. A train pulled in as I reached the ramp, and I was in the office in twenty minutes. I used a typewriter at the back of a large newsroom, near the windows from which you could almost touch the El tracks. I carried the story up to the desk myself."[22] But the point of view often switches from that of Silver to the two boys. Unlike Levin's earlier attempts at a complex handling of point of view, the dual perspective of *Compulsion* is neither confusing nor damaging to the continuity of the story. The narrator-novelist comes and goes as would a good reporter. When he is on the scene, the reader experiences with him the dramatic unfolding of events. During the flashbacks, however, the narrator distances himself in order to observe, record, and focus. All this is done in a rather sophisticated and effective manner, as psychology becomes juxtaposed with drama, and inner thoughts with actual deeds.

The style is also Levin at his best: fiction and fact flow easily together, though not so readily as to make it difficult to distinguish one from the other. The prose is generally that of good investigative reporting, although Levin occasionally feels the need to interrupt the otherwise fast-moving pace of the narrative with his subjective comments. The language is mostly realistic and the dialogue is explicit. As a result, the novel was criticized by some for its vulgarity. But the scatalogical imagery and the explicit accounts of sexuality serve an express purpose in the novel: without this authentic background there would be no clear picture of the private world of the two pathological killers.

Like *Citizens* and *The Old Bunch*, the novel is a realistic rendering of events, mood, and atmosphere. The emotional climate of the community, the shock and dismay and despair of the families of the two young men, as well as the crime itself are recreated with accuracy and an understanding of the many conflicting factors involved. The story is fascinating, and the narration sustains and supports the inherent drama of the crime and subsequent trial. Essential, however, to Levin's purposes, was an understanding of the deviant personalities of the two intellectual criminals themselves.

Characters. Although the action is taken from real events, Levin used fictional names throughout because, as he stated, "It must be recognized that thoughts and emotions described in the characters come from within the author, as he imagines them to belong to the personages in the case he has chosen" (vii–viii). By not using the names of those involved in the case, Levin allowed himself the freedom to transcend actual events in order to discover inner feelings and to speculate as to motivations. The characters of Judd Steiner (Leopold) and Artie Strauss (Loeb) emerge through their backgrounds and the events that might have helped shape their personalities: the influence of governesses and doting yet distant parents, sibling jealousies, and experiments with homosexuality. Based on what he found in the psychiatric reports of the trial, for example, Levin was able to dramatize Leopold's recurrent king and slave fantasies, in which he was sometimes the king, sometimes the slave. Similarly, he was able to reconstruct Loeb's daydream of becoming a criminal mastermind. The boys' conversations with each other were realistically imagined, as were the debates with university professors that helped shape their poorly conceived philosophy of the Nietzsche *Ubermensch*: " 'But granted that the law applies to the ordinary person in society,' Judd said, 'how would it apply in the case of the superman? The concept of an *Ubermensch* in itself means that he must be above ordinary society. If he abided by ordinary laws he could never produce the actions that might in the end prove of the greatest benefit to humanity—not that even benefit to humanity should be a criterion' " (5).

Judd and Artie are portrayed as brilliant yet inept, diabolical yet often infantile and childlike. Individually they appear incapable of kidnap and murder; but together, as friends and as lovers, they see themselves as superior, Nietzschean wonders on whom it was impossible to fix moral guilt. It is only through their close association that their mutually dependent egos are fed to the point that they can conceive of and actualize their crime. In the classroom, as in all phases of their existence, their inflated sense of self is maintained only through the presence of the other: "Judd only wished Artie were here with him now, so they could share a quick wink, listening to McKinnon's platitudes. At some particularly banal remark he would touch his knee against Artie's, and Artie would turn his face and wink" (3).

When the boys are finally arrested and brought to trial, their arrogance is barely abated. In the custody of the police and in the courtroom, Judd and Artie are pictured as aloof, superior, often bored with the proceedings: "For Judd, the trial was the last bitter irony. Was this the great trial that was in a sense to have justified his crime by bringing momentous questions before mankind? The question of free will, the question of law and the superman, reduced to routine evidence about a fake signature on a hotel registry. And for Artie, there was no particular disappointment, only boredom; to him the outcome was interesting only as a kind of bet, a long shot on life" (392). When the sentence is finally handed down—life imprisonment for murder, an additional ninety-nine years for kidnapping, with a recommendation of no parole—there is little reaction from either Judd or Artie; and Levin declines to speculate on what, if any, their emotions were at that moment.

Despite Levin's penetrating analysis of the two boys, perhaps the most memorable figure in the novel is that of Clarence Darrow (given the fictional name of Jonathan Wilk), who was seventy at the time of the trial. Levin draws a convincing portrait of Darrow and his commanding presence in the agitated Chicago courtroom of August 1924. His concluding speech (cited verbatim from the court records) is a masterpiece of pleading for the social outcast. The oration, included in its entirety, becomes the high-point of part 2 and the philosophical center of the novel, serving both as summary and as explanation of the crime that Levin believed "epitomized the thinking" of an entire generation.

The characterization of Darrow, however, functions more as a symbol than as a living entity; for the lawyer, in all his grandeur and brilliance, personified Levin's ultimate condemnation of Leopold and Loeb and their doctrine of the superman. In the legendary figure of Darrow, Levin saw an example of a truly superior person, not an egotist, nor one who was above moral law, but rather as an individual who had achieved his greatest possible potential: "One might have wondered if he were not some example of the superior man, hardly in the arrogant sense, but a man . . . who cast a spell of tragic nobility, of faith through his very pessimism; it was in him that might have been read the possibility in every man to become something more than himself" (488).

Theme. Part 2, "The Trial of the Century," develops the main theme of the novel: the existential questions of individual responsibility and free will. Levin's immediate purpose was to ascertain the psychological motivation of the two boys. On a wider level, however, he wished to interpret those forces that lay behind the murder in terms of contemporary society. For him the act was more than that of individual psychopaths acting in a vacuum, but was rather indicative of a whole generation: "Certain crimes seem to epitomize the thinking of their era. Thus *Crime and Punishment* had to arise out of the feverish soul-searching of the Russia of Dostoevski's period, and *An American Tragedy* had to arise from the sociological thinking of Dreiser's time in America. In our time, the psychoanalytical point of view has come to the fore" (vii).

Levin suggests that there is a link between the thinking of the boys—their intellectuality, the impersonal nature of their crime, the dominance of their egos—and that of the collective mood of contemporary America. Levin (and the attorneys for the defense) claimed that Leopold and Loeb were the products of a sick society rather than its deviants. From this emanated the frightening thought that the potential for crime and even murder resided in all of America's children, and that the murder itself was a reflection of some collective guilt. The explicit suggestion that any child, despite his family background, had the potential for criminal behavior becomes the focal point of Darrow's plea to save the lives of the two boys: "If I should succeed in saving these boys' lives and do nothing for the progress of the law, I should feel sad indeed. If I can succeed, my greatest reward and my greater hope will be that I have done something for the tens and thousands of other boys, for the countless unfortunates who must tread the same road in blind childhood that these boys have trod—that I have done something to help human understanding" (490). The implication is clear, and Levin retells the Leopold and Loeb story as much to teach us about ourselves as to recreate the dramatic crime of the century.

Conclusion. In spite of Levin's hope for universality, *Compulsion* succeeds, not so much as a novel that reveals the American psyche and determines the metaphysical ills of our society, but as a graphic and absorbing reconstruction of an infamous and psychologically complex crime. The novel is significant because of

Levin's concern for his story, his attention to detail, and his understanding of the importance of all the factors surrounding the crime and subsequent trial. The "realism" of *Compulsion* is of a higher order than that of, say, *Citizens* or *The New Bridge,* for here Levin accomplished what he had attempted in his earlier novels but rarely achieved: an intermingling of subjective and objective reality. The story told by Levin is one of imagined history; he has recreated the events through his own experience and involvement, as well as from the added insight of a mature artist.

Although *Compulsion* succeeds on many counts, it fails on several others. Levin's prose is often appropriate and integral to the novel's action and structure. At other times it is painfully awkward and stumbling, especially in his attempts to capture the language heard around the University of Chicago during the 1920s. Levin's constant authorial intrusion is also a serious distraction. The terms that he uses are now familiar to any student of introductory psychology, and the tone of his explanations is unnecessarily pretentious and didactic: "Then, when he was nine, Artie's little brother Billy was born. Today we all are aware of the intense difficulty this can make for a child at about this age, though surely not everyone who has a baby brother at nine turns out to be a murderer" (355).

Despite these weaknesses, the novel remains highly readable and one of Levin's most satisfying works. The critics, although quick to point out the book's shortcomings, were generally in agreement about Levin's fine effort. Erle Stanley Gardner, writing in the *New York Times Book Review* (28 October 1956), called *Compulsion* "a masterly achievement in literary craftsmanship, . . . a frightening book because the author has such an uncanny ability to make the dark recesses of perverted abnormality seem so thoroughly logical." And Rose Feld, in the *New York Herald Tribune* (28 October 1956), called it "a book which can take its place with Dreiser's *An American Tragedy.*" There was, of course, much discussion and some condemnation of Levin's use of profanity and his explicit description of sexual activities. The *Chicago*

Sunday Tribune (28 October 1956), for instance, claimed that Levin "sacrifices taste to shock" and went on to state: "Many writers have written of degeneracy with an economy of words. Levin uses many words, most of them dirty ones."

Largely due to the coarse language and the sensational subject matter, which were objectionable to many editors, the novel was rejected several times before it found a home at Simon and Schuster. Published in 1956, *Compulsion* was an immediate commercial success. The hard-cover edition sold close to 150,000 copies; the paperback edition, published in 1958, has gone through seven printings to date.[23] No other book was to make Levin as well-known; no other work was to be as financially rewarding. Just turning fifty Levin was able, for the first time, to give up his scramble for a living. He was now an independent writer, capable of sustaining himself as such: "For the first time in my life I had real money. . . . For a few months I could hardly adjust to it. . . . I was afraid to spend money. And I didn't really have too much to spend, as in the contract I had limited myself to an annual stipend, thinking that if the book should be a hit, I might never have another one again. Indeed, none of the books that followed in the next fifteen years earned enough to cover the time of writing."[24]

Levin's mood of elation was short-lived. The success of his novel had changed little in terms of his frustration and struggle over *The Diary*. The case was soon to come to trial, and Levin believed that a successful Broadway play of his own would help convince the court that his detractors were wrong, that he was indeed capable of writing an actable play. Levin began to conceive of a dramatization of *Compulsion*; the idea was sold to a producer. Levin wrote the script only to have the producer call in another author to make what he thought to be small but necessary adjustments. A distraught Levin protested; the changes, it seemed to him, were not incidental but essential to the integrity of the play. He asked for a Theatre Guild arbitration to rule on the producer's right to tamper with his script, which was followed by a special court arbitration. Despite the fact that the judge ruled that all textual modification had to be justified and argued in his presence, Levin eventually dropped the case (weary of still more court appearances) and allowed the revised version to be produced. Wanting, however, to divorce himself from what he believed to be a vulgarization of his original work, Levin required the program to state that this was the "producer's version" of a dramatization by Meyer Levin.

The show lasted four months on Broadway: not a tremendous hit, but certainly not a failure either. But for Levin, the ordeal was one that only added to his already growing bitterness and disappointment over the Anne Frank incident. Although the original play was later produced successfully by drama companies in other parts of the country, and although the work was published in 1959 by Simon and Schuster (with an acrimonious forward by Levin stating his case against the producers and the powers of commercialism), *Compulsion, A Play* remains a forgotten work.

Chapter Five
The Aftermath of War

After the publication of *Compulsion*, Levin settled more or less permanently in Israel with his second wife, the novelist Tereska Torres. Except for short visits and lecture tours in the United States, he remained in his adopted country for the rest of his life. In the years that followed *Compulsion* Levin wrote three interesting—if not completely successful—books, each dealing in various ways with the subject of the holocaust and its aftermath. *Eva* (1959) is a documentary novel of a Jewish girl's experience during the Nazi reign of terror and her difficult adjustment to life after the concentration camp. *The Fanatic* (1963) is told through the imagined consciousness of a *dybbuk* (a soul trapped between the world of the living and the dead), a poet and victim of the Nazis who returns to examine several past and present moral issues. *The Stronghold* (1965), which takes place in a German fortress and prison for high-ranking European and Jewish officials, is a philosophical inquest into the theme of human and divine responsibility. The three novels cannot be called a trilogy, for they represent different viewpoints and subject matter. Thematically, however, they share a concern for the large moral and social issues of the holocaust; they are three distinct works that nevertheless have similar objectives.

Eva

Levin arrived in Israel still preoccupied with *The Diary* case and still bitter over the dramatization of *Compulsion*. He had hoped to begin work on a project that he had long envisioned: the story of a pioneer family in Palestine. The events of the recent past, however, had left him frustrated and hopelessly "blocked." Then came a letter from an Israeli woman, an immigrant from Poland by the name of Ida Lev, who had read about the American Jewish author's arrival in Tel Aviv. For years she had wanted to tell her story of survival and escape from Hitler's death camps and to purge once and for all her obsessive need to articulate the horror of her past. She decided to write to Levin in the hope that he would listen to her story and give it proper expression. Her letter was short and direct. "I am a survivor," she wrote, "I have survived everything. It began when I ran away from Poland, and became someone altogether different. Another girl with another name and another faith."[1]

Levin had received several similar letters during his first months in Israel. There were, it seemed, many people who, like Ida, carried around their stories of tragedy inside themselves and longed to be relieved of their burdens. But something touching yet forceful came from Ida's letter, and Levin answered. This led to a personal meeting and ultimately a decision to undertake the project.

Ida wanted the book to be exact. At first Levin used her real name and those of other people involved, many of them alive and living in Israel. Gradually, however, the demands of the present began to outweigh those of the past, and Ida Lev's story became the story of her fictional counterpart, Eva Korngold.

Eva (1959) therefore, like *Compulsion*, is a documentary novel. It recounts the actual experiences of Ida Lev during World War II. Told in the first person, it is the story of a Jewish girl who flees Nazi occupied Poland disguised as a Ukranian peasant. Under an assumed name she works as a domestic in Vienna, then as a government worker in a munitions plant, until she is eventually discovered by the Gestapo and sent to Auschwitz. After several years of hard labor, she miraculously escapes and gradually, with great difficulty, makes her way to safety in Palestine. But the novel is as much the story of her inner struggle to preserve her spirit and dignity, as it is the chronicle of her physical battle to survive.

In *Compulsion* Levin moved from the particular to the general, raising an abnormal individual situation to the level of universal significance. In *Eva* he reverses the process, reducing the history of the entire holocaust to the microcosm of a single human being. That individual is Eva Korngold, a pretty Jewish girl in her late teens who has grown up in a small Polish town. Naive and innocent, she is virtually ignorant of events outside her small community. Nevertheless, when the Jews of her own town are threatened by the oncoming Nazis, she is forced to flee. Her mother, with tears in her eyes and old family joke on her lips, bids Eva farewell: " 'You have been a good daughter, even if you were such a wild one.' She wiped a tear and repeated, sniffing, her habitual, joking 'curse,' the 'curse' she bestowed on me whenever I was at my worst. 'May your own children be as wild as you are, and pay you back!' And then she whispered, 'Live, my daughter. Live.' "[2]

By necessity, Eva begins a life filled with guile and deceit. Assuming the name of Katarina Leszezyszyn, she poses as a Ukranian Catholic and is able to live out a major part of the war in Austria. Levin's early characterization of Eva as simple and artless sometimes makes it hard to believe she is so successful at her subterfuge. But successful she is. Faced with a crisis, Eva bcomes as devious and cunning as a master criminal. She acquires false papers, learns to recite the "Hail Mary" and to shout "Heil Hitler." Although she works for an overtly anti-Semitic family, she never errs in her masquerade. At one point she is actually certified as an Aryan after a minute examination by a Gestapo committee and is even invited by the Nazis to report on another similarly disguised Jew.

All this subterfuge laces the story with considerable intrigue. But Levin develops another aspect of the narrative as well. Eva is an attractive girl, vulnerable and lonely, yearning to grow and live like a woman. She eventually forms a romantic attachment to a young Czechoslovakian and, in an unusually careless gesture, gives away her secret to him. She also tempts fate by regularly visiting a Jewish girl friend who is similarly duping the Germans—and even speaks in Yiddish, the forbidden language.

It is, of course, this negligence that finally leads to her discovery and capture. Eva is sent to Auschwitz and assigned, not to the crematorium, but to hard labor. From this point on the tone of the novel changes, as suspense and drama give way to a mood of horror and despair. Eva describes with grim pathos the life of the barracks: the meager rations of bread and watery soup, the foul toilets, and perhaps most harrowing of all, the "mussulmans," the living dead of Auschwitz:

> Among the "normal" prisoners, the emaciated but yet enduring, there were a number of skeletal beings with faces of a peculiar kind, faces in which the light of the spirit was entirely absent; only a kind of existing remnant of the body was there, of an organism not yet dead. There was a look in their eyes—or, rather, a vacancy. Of all that I had seen until then, these faces brought the deepest despair to me. These, I knew, were the creatures called mussulmans, the creatures in the last stage, when they reacted only as brute animals. Sometimes they could cling to existence for months in this state, before dying. (223–24)

Despite the horror around her, Eva manages to survive and finally, during a midnight death march, to escape.

The last section of the novel describes Eva's flight from behind the Nazi lines and her long underground trek to safety in Palestine. The book ends with Eva in Israel, married and the mother of two sons. Now in Tel Aviv, she has at long last joined the living and the contented: "I like it best when I just catch a glimpse of one of my friends going about her life, perhaps going into a shop somewhere. And I say to myself, Why, she looks like an everyday housewife living her ordinary life. You'd never imagine what she's been through. And then I find myself thinking, You, too, Eva! That's what you must look like, too! And I feel content" (311).

Levin tells his story in the first person, a difficult task to perform when the sex of the narrator is not that of the author. But he succeeds in adopting the feminine point of view and thus conveying his heroine's essential humanity as well as her inherent femininity. Eva's personality is portrayed honestly and perceptively. She is shown in her many phases of womanhood: as a teenager, a young woman in love, a prisoner determined to survive, and a mother. Levin's ability to portray Eva's need to function as a woman is perhaps his greatest achievement in the novel. As critic Marghanita Laski, writing for the *Saturday Review* (29 August 1959), observed: "He is so deeply aware of the essential humanity of her situation that even when he is, as he sometimes must be, specific about feminine feelings and functions, the reader accepts *this* knowledge of her because all his other knowledge of Eva has proved acceptable. Indeed, if the good writer must be, as Virginia Woolf suggests, androgynous, Mr. Levin shows himself singlarly well equipped with womanly penetration."

While Levin succeeds in presenting a convincing portrait of his female protagonist, he fails to overcome other problems posed by the device of a first-person narration. Since the whole story is recounted by Eva herself, it necessarily reflects her limited knowledge, outlook, and mentality. The result is a narration that is, despite its exciting moments and despite the moving descriptions of concentration camp life, rather drab and colorless. The problem goes beyond style as well, for the monotonous tone of the novel ultimately mitigates the force of Eva's shattering experience.

The most serious failing of the novel, however, is neither stylistic nor structural. *Eva* is a book that attempts to portray a tragedy of enormous proportions. Nevertheless, it is a novel of survival with a happy conclusion. The story of Eva's triumph is, as we know, authentic, and surely there are many others who survived the holocaust to live satisfying lives. But aesthetically Levin is working at cross purposes. On the one hand, he wants his readers to grasp the massive destruction of the holocaust; on the other hand, he conveys that experience in clearly optimistic terms.

One's emotional involvement, as one reads *Eva*, is with the survivors rather than with those who perished. Gradually the reader begins to lose sight of the horror of the concentration camp, since Levin's heroine endures and triumphs. Survival is a happy ending, and Levin's vision is not sufficiently profound to make us feel the monstrous price a people had to pay for that survival.

The Fanatic

"I have always," Levin wrote in the foreward to *The Fanatic* (1963), "been the sort of writer who receives his impulse from life."[3] The more one comes to know Levin's creative process, the more one realizes that his fiction, as he states, is not so much created as reproduced from life. Levin's greatest literary accomplishments have been a combination of his use of realistic detail and his ability to transform and purify experience through his creative imagination. Rarely, however, is the factual base so clearly apprehended as in *The Fanatic*, and rarely does the event function so completely to serve a preconceived thesis. The novel is a retelling, only thinly disguised with fictional names, of Levin's own experience with *The Diary of a Young Girl.* There is little universal application of these facts—as there was in *Compulsion* and *Citizens*—and only a feeble attempt to draw upon their significance for the rest of us. *The Fanatic*, unfortunately, functions more as vendetta than as fiction.

Eva, Compulsion, and *Citizens* are all stories that have their foundation in fact and historical event. But these novels, as a result of Levin's art and his ability to link the general with the specific, exist on their own. If in *Compulsion*, for instance, the reader has the background to be able to substitute real names for those of Judd Steiner, Artie Strauss, and others who figured in the murder and trial, it brings an added dimension to the reading. But it is not necessary; *Compulsion* stands firmly on its own as a work of fiction. Such is not the case with *The Fanatic*. The facts follow too closely those of Levin's own story without the benefit of objective observation. Levin's foreword, with its insistence that the novel is fiction, only serves to reinforce our idea to the contrary. The reader who is at all familiar with Levin's difficulties during this time cannot resist translating fiction into fact. "It is essential to me," Levin claims, "that the reader approach this story to seek ideas, meanings, beliefs rather than to seek personal histories" (8). The personal, however, is rendered in such a way as to subsume all other issues. The tone is one of self-pity, and the reader feels manipulated to respond to the injustice done to the author. Levin does not write from the desire to explore or penetrate, but from a personal need to analyze and exorcise his own obsession. Thus what purports to be a novel concerned with the most important moral issues, becomes merely topical, and ultimately *The Fanatic* adheres more to Levin's need for cartharsis than to the demands of good fiction.

Levin's central character and the fanatic of the title is Maury Finkelstein, a young rabbi turned playwright, whose story is narrated by the dead Leo Kahn. Leo's story is interesting, although mostly incidental to the novel's theme. The son of a renowned Czechoslovakian professor and scholar of Jewish mysticism, Leo was arrested at the start of Hitler's reign of terror and sent to a Nazi death camp. Once there, he managed to escape and return home in order to warn the remaining Jews of their awaiting fate. Ignored by his fellow townspeople, Leo was arrested a second time and sent back to the death camp where he eventually perished. He left a legacy, however, a penetrating and moving manuscript (we are told) about the Jews and their extermination by the Nazis. Part fiction, part philosophical dialogue, *Good and Evil*—as the tract is entitled—is, it seems, a haunting and intelligent document waiting to be discovered.

Maury Finkelstein, whose fate eventually becomes linked with that of Leo Kahn, is bookish, insecure, and uncertain of his religious commitment. Steeped in the social and cultural life of New

York City's Jewish ghetto, he becomes a rabbi due to the urgings of his mother and uncle and in spite of his own agnosticism. Maury, a rather sad and inept figure, is driven by his creative forces and consumed by the need to dramatize his own experiences. As a rabbi, he hopes to have time to write. True to his inner promptings, he avoids the responsibilities of a congregation and writes religious plays—about the prophet Elijah, the eternal diaspora of the Jews, and the life of Moses. In spite of his religious skepticism, a new sense of Jewish identity begins to come over him, one that is linked to his writing and the entire cultural past of his people. At the outbreak of World War II, his plays help raise funds to rescue Jews from Nazi Germany. When the United States finally enters the war, he immediately volunteers and is assigned to the chaplain service on the European front.

Here too, however, Maury eschews the pulpit and spends his time locating Jewish refugees and helping them to reestablish their broken lives. At the war's end he travels from one concentration camp to the next, attempting to rescue survivors and place them in contact with relatives. (Levin, of course, had performed a similar task.) One day Maury travels to Terezin to look for the famed Professor David Kahn, whose writing he had studied in the seminary. The professor, like his son, has perished; but his wife has survived, and she shows him Leo's manuscript.

Purely by chance Maury's present life becomes more and more intertwined with Leo Kahn's past. He meets Leo's fiancée Anika, falls in love, and brings her to America to be his wife. He also becomes fascinated with *Good and Evil*, which Leo's mother has finally succeeded in publishing in a limited German edition.

Once in America, Maury works for publication of an English translation of the work. Convinced of the great stage possibilities of the book, he secures the dramatization rights from Leo's mother. Here, Maury thinks, is the essential work he has been waiting for all his life: the story of Jewish martyrdom under the Nazis, the undying Jewish hope for a homeland, and philosophical speculation about the relationship of God to the six million dead. The book is published in the United States, although not directly as a result of Maury's efforts. Nevertheless, he writes a stage version of *Good and Evil* and eagerly seeks production. The book, however, has turned into a worldwide best-seller, and commercial and political forces begin to move in against the relatively unknown dramatist. The play is taken away from him; legal battles ensue over the rights. In the meantime, an adulterated version is produced on Broadway, its Jewish content reduced to an incidental feature, its essential Zionist theme replaced by the message of internationalism. Maury begins an obsessive fight for justice against overwhelming odds. He sees his struggle not only as one of personal vindication, not only as the preservation of the original spirit of Leo Kahn's work, but also as a symbolic fight for artistic freedom and individual rights. Maury's obsessive need for justice becomes foremost in his life. He succeeds in alienating all his former supporters. Every part of his life is touched and damaged—his health, his marriage, even a second play he has written, entitled, without subtlety, *Job*. Maury becomes a solitary figure facing a solid wall of adversaries, which includes producers, lawyers, the press, even Leo's mother and her new husband. His life is in shambles; yet he continues, doggedly hounding people to death, circulating petitions, filing suits, and holding press conferences of his own. After a long and exhausting struggle, Maury finally wins a small victory in court. Although he is somewhat vindicated, recompense is too late and too little to outweigh the enormous personal damage that he has endured.

Maury's saga of suffering and tribulation is told from the point of view of the dead Leo Kahn, whose support for Maury is unequivocal. Leo's voice comes from the mass grave of the six million. By using the device of the dead narrator (and specifically one who perished in the holocaust), Levin intended to raise his story above the level of the personal and give it wider meaning. But Leo's musing over Broadway infighting and his championing of Maury's cause appear, in view of his tragic stance, inappropriate. By associating the martyrdom of Leo with that of Maury, Levin trivializes Leo's fate and, by extension, that of the victims of the holocaust. Furthermore, Leo Kahn is a figure from beyond the grave and not a character with whom one can easily identify. Whereas in *Compulsion*, Levin created a sympathetic (albeit autobiographical) narrator one could follow comfortably throughout the story, *The Fanatic* has no such guide. The events of *Compulsion* are told with detachment and with an eye toward discovering the universal significance of the event for the modern reader. Leo Kahn is neither objective nor capable of translating the importance of this particular set of circumstances for the reader. The existence of his transcendent voice is not sufficient to dispel the notion that Levin is writing from a personal sense of grievance, rather than from the need to explore the ethical and moral questions that are only superficially posed.

There are other weaknesses in *The Fanatic*, most of them a result of Levin's limited sense of purpose. The book's style, for example, is controlled (as are almost all other elements) by Levin's indignation. The language—mostly the rhetoric of anger and protest—is melodramatic and calculated to evoke reader response; as, for instance, this conversation between Maury and Anika: " 'Maury, they aren't worthy of you!' she cries. And as she sees angry tears well up in his eyes, her own tears come, and she is in his arms. . . . 'The hypocrites, the rotten hypocrites!'. . . 'I fought all I could, to hell with them, the hell with the lot of them! To let such people destroy us' " (259). Despite these frequent outbursts, there is little excitement or drama in the novel. Events move slowly, and the story proceeds tediously and humorlessly throughout its almost five hundred pages.

More significantly, neither the novel's characters nor its plot develop from any inner necessity, but are manipulated to produce Levin's predetermined objective. *The Fanatic* is peopled with good guys and bad guys. The cards are unconvincingly stacked against

Maury's enemies, who all seem to personify the very worst of the capitalist system—men and women of power, greed, and dishonesty. Typically, they vilify Maury at every opportunity: " 'He is the last sonofabitch in the world to do this play!' " the producer of *Good and Evil* is told by his theatrical advisor; " 'That rabbi bastard has a nose, he smelled out the book way back in Europe; he even married Leo Kahn's girl when he thought she had a finger on the rights' " (156).

Levin's one fine achievement in the novel is his convincing portrait of Maury and his obsessive/compulsive behavior. As the novel unfolds, it becomes clear that Maury is authentically and painfully tormented, not only by the outrages committed against him, but also by his awareness that his own response is exaggerated and neurotic. Where, Maury begins to ask himself, does reality end and paranoia take over? As Maury's fate worsens, he cannot be sure if his passion for justice has been supplanted by his appetite for vindication and revenge. His motives derive from both principle and ego, and he can never be certain which dominates: "What began as good will and heroism in the world, with love for a cause, ends in a betrayal, in a personal wound, and festers, and becomes a malformation, a thing in itself, an obsession" (222). Maury is clearly moving toward madness, and the knowledge that Levin too might have been descending a similar path gives *The Fanatic* a tone of ingenuousness that it would not otherwise possess.

A decade later, Levin, still obviously "obsessed" with *The Diary* incident, tried again to "write it out." *The Obsession* (1973) is a more poignant and moving book because it deals with the case on more honest (and openly autobiographical) terms. Levin portrays his torment with a good deal of self-indulgence, but without the pretense of concern with the universal problems of man. *The Fanatic*, by comparison, presumes to be preoccupied with the great issues of its time but ultimately treats only the personal details and travail of the author's own life, a shortcoming that accounts for the fact that *The Fanatic* is one of Levin's lesser achievements.

The Stronghold

Several decades after the war, Levin, like other writers who chose to remember the horror of the concentration camps, began to see how easily the Nazi campaign of extermination dissolved into the realm of myth and legend. As one of the characters in *The Stronghold* (1965) attests: "The vastness of it was too much for the human psyche to accept."[4] Twenty years after the fact, the memory of the event had begun to be extinguished. Levin's intention, in what was to be his final treatment of the holocaust theme, was to bring the "legend" to life and force people once again to remember the horror and destruction, and the death of six million Jews. Like *Eva, The Stronghold* reduces the enormous proportions of the holocaust to human terms and to the microcosm of individual lives.

The story, set in a castle somewhere in Bavaria, is about a group of (presumably French) prisoners—a politician and his mistress, a soldier, a priest, and a journalist—held by the Germans. The time is the last days of World War II; the advancing Allies are only a few miles away. Although most of the German soldiers still cling to the hope of a sudden reversal of events, there is one Nazi officer who is very much aware that defeat is imminent and who begins to plan for his own safety. He is *Obersturmbannfuerhrer* Kraus, the archetypal S.S. officer, an Adolph Eichmann-like character who has been largely responsible, although mostly unrewarded, for the implementation of the "final solution" to the Jewish problem. Escaping the onslaught of the approaching troops, Krauss makes his way to the castle with two vivid reminders of his role in the war: a strongbox filled with valuables pilfered from Jewish corpses—wedding rings, jewelry, gold dental fillings—and a Jewish ex-head of state, saved from the gas ovens by Kraus to serve his future purposes. Paul

Vered, a man with a strong resemblance to Leon Blum, is one of the most important political prisoners of the war and therefore an excellent hostage.

Once inside the fortress, Kraus takes command and offers freedom to his captives in exchange for a letter attesting to his ethical conduct—a statement that would absolve him of all war crimes. The bargain is tempting to the prisoners, of whom only Vered is a Jew who has suffered traumatically at the hands of the Nazis. But when the others learn from Vered the full horror of the concentration camps and the realities of the extermination program, they refuse Kraus's offer at the risk of death. Their deliberations dominate the first half of the novel and reveal the entire spectrum of attitudes towards the Jews and the war.

In the second half, philosophical discussion gives way to a drama of action and violence. Kraus is eventually overcome by the prisoners with the aid of the baron of the castle, who assumes his future safety to be with the allies. Instead of keeping Kraus prisoner, however, the baron allows him to leave, believing that Kraus wishes only to return to his family for one final reunion before surrender. But Kraus is not so easily dissuaded from his original objective. Assembling a small group of Nazi soldiers and a Panzer tank, he returns to the castle to recapture the prisoners and his precious strongbox. His attack fails, although one of the prisoners is killed in an effort to destroy the Panzer, and Kraus is able to plant a mine which eventually (and ironically) kills two Jewish members of the approaching American forces. About the time the prisoners are successfully holding off Kraus's attack, the Americans arrive to liberate the fortress and bring the prisoners to safety. Kraus, however, somehow manages to escape in the confusion.

Levin always had a gift for storytelling, and here the hour-by-hour action of the novel, with its sudden reversals and unexpected turns, is well rendered. The novel's unique achievement is its fusion of the dramatic and philosophical. Whereas in *The Fanatic,* Levin obviously manipulated characters and events to demonstrate a preconceived thesis, the structure of the story here seems to advance the development of central motifs and ideas. The philosophical debate that takes place as the action unfolds functions within the narrative, rather than separate from it, and hence thematic concerns are well integrated with plot structure.

The issues that Levin raises—the charges of Christ-killing, divided loyalties, the origin of anti-Semitism—are by no means new, and few answers are offered. But the debates and discussions are rendered in fast, provocative dialogue, and the issues are treated seriously and with intelligence. Foremost among these is the question of anti-Semitism and its many ramifications, not only in terms of the Nazi regime, but throughout history. The novel aims at firmly destroying the notion that a few top-ranking war criminals were wholly responsible for the extermination of millions of Jews. The guilt, Levin claims, must be shared by the entire German (and even non-German) population, the educated and the uneducated, the military and the nonmilitary. Each of the characters functions to expose some aspect of this shared guilt. Kraus, for example, is representative of the anti-Semite of low social origins and of limited mental capabilities. Essentially stupid, extremely dangerous because of his blind loyalty to a misguided ideal, he is the embodiment of what Hannah Arendt called the "banality of evil." We are given little insight into the genesis of his hatred; we are told that his becoming a member of the S.S. was somewhat by chance, largely due to the urging of his wife to "specialize." He is addicted to violence and finds in it the fulfillment of his personality: "He moved forward, his hands touching his tools of attack to make certain he was ready. What he did here was an integral part of his existence. To emerge from the war years and return without having struck one direct blow at the enemy would have left him without a sense of his right to speak, to lead" (292).

As a caricature of a Nazi officer, Kraus is an effective mouthpiece of Hitlerian rhetoric. As a fictional character, however, he is one-dimensional, functioning only as a representative type.

Levin's characterization of Kraus contains no psychological depth and no distinguishing qualities that would somehow make him come alive as a complex individual rather than a puppet villain. Levin allows his readers no insight into the dynamics of Kraus's hatred. He serves Levin's purpose as the composite Nazi. His actions and his speech are contrived to provoke a calculated response: "If Kraus caught so much as a glint of this in the Jew-devil's eye . . . enough! He'd have Gunter halt the car, drag out the old carcass and make a corpse of him. He ought to do it anyway. . . . The Jew Premier! . . . What a sign it was of the enemy's degeneracy to have made a Jew their chief of state" (12–13).

Somewhat better realized is the aged baron, lord of the castle and counterpart to Kraus's unthinking prejudice. The baron's attitude toward "the Jewish question" is somewhat more complex than the brutal and simplistic hatred of Kraus, although no less pernicious. He stands for a type of German—or non-German for that matter—who is "personally quite rational," but nevertheless secure in the knowledge of his own racial superiority. His world view is archaic and perversely romantic. He refers to Hitler as "the loved one," and interprets the campaign of extermination as a "romantic urge for a perfectly ordered society" (83). Behaving with icy correctness toward the prisoners, the baron thrives on visions of Germany as a land of order and beauty: "A nation, a folk, all knights, all rulers! The vision of ordered beauty as in ancient Greece, of ordered mastery as in ancient Rome, heightened and extended, projected into the realm of machine power with only the *Herrenvolk* as masters of the machines" (304).

Among the prisoners there exists another type of discrimination against the Jews, less visible and perhaps less vicious, but evident nevertheless. Although Vered's fellow politicians had never considered him Jewish "in the pejorative sense," they too had always accepted certain anti-Semitic beliefs: "Of course the marshal had known that the epithet, Jew, had been applied to Paul Vered, as he had known that the Premier was a Jew by birth, though fortunately of an old distinguished family. . . . Naturally he did not care for the Jews, as Jews. . . . If there were some officers who were Jews by birth they were, like Vered, persons who simply were not 'Jews' in the pejorative sense" (250–51). As the discussion among the prisoners progresses and further attitudes toward the Jews and the war are revealed, the marshal, a former politician, begins to comprehend that his presumably innocuous sentiments could somehow be linked to the Nazi hatred of Jews and that Paul Vered had been singled out for persecution, not because of his position in the fallen government, but because of his religion.

The novel's central theme of the ubiquity of anti-Semitism is furthered by the deliberations of another prisoner, Frère Luc. A "social action priest," Luc reluctantly comes to the conclusion that hatred of the Jews did not begin with the rise of the Third Reich and would certainly not end with its demise. Looking back on his own education and the teachings of the church, Luc begins to accept the fact that the guilt for mass genocide must be shared by the church and its two thousand years of dogma that has portrayed the Jews as killers of Christ, and even perhaps by Christ himself. "Why had the Christ of the Church," Luc asks, "why had the Christ of universal love, remained silent in all this holocaust, until there were Christians that could believe it was His will?" (186).

Just as the non-Jews in the castle examine their attitudes toward the Jews, Vered, the only Jew present, begins to ponder his role in a Christian society. An assimilationist and a former prime minister, Vered was a man "who all his life had felt only the most tenuous involvement with his origin" (98). He had naively believed himself to be insulated against exclusion and racial hatred. But when the Nazis invade and conquer his country, he is imprisoned, and his wife is sent to the gas chamber. When Vered emerges from the concentration camp, he is left with a new and painfully acquired awareness of what it means to be a Jew. He can experience neither joy nor relief that he has survived, but only guilt in the knowledge that he, in his old age, was chosen to live while so many millions perished. "You have no right," he tells himself, "or even wish, to escape the fate of the Jews" (252).

The issue of the destiny of the Jews is linked to the allegorical framework of the novel—the conflict between good and evil. Throughout the action the forces of good, personified by the Christ-like figure of Vered, struggle against the Satanic figure of Kraus. Despite Levin's passionately moral point of view, there is no clear victor in this battle. The Germans are defeated, but when the Americans finally liberate the castle, Kraus has mysteriously disappeared. "Does not the Gospel tell us," Frère Luc intones at the conclusion of the novel, "that there will be wars until the evil in man is conquered" (317). And Levin clearly points to this private Armageddon as only one step in man's struggle against the forces of evil and destruction.

There are few religious or ethical questions that are not raised in the novel: the existence of good and evil, the will of God, human suffering, the responsibility of the church, and the responsibility of the individual. Many of these issues seem to be superficially presented, for the novel attempts to encompass too great a metaphysical panorama. Problems are put forth, but none are resolved. The novel closes with a series of rhetorical questions: "What can a man do? What can I do? What must I do? . . . Because of what, then? Of whom? . . . Of existence itself? Of God?" (318–19). Appearing at the end of the novel, much of this is gratuitous; but Levin is not, at least, guilty of providing facile solutions. The existential confrontation between the philosophy of nihilism and that of belief, which is at the base of all religious experience, is illustrated in personal and human terms. Unlike *Eva,* there are no happy endings in this novel, and the reader is left to examine the difficult issues raised in the solitude of his own "stronghold."

If one comes to *The Stronghold* after either *Eva* or *The Fanatic,* one is refreshed. By comparison, it is a well conceived work—economical in its structure, realistic in its dialogue, and interesting in its philosophical reflections. The novel's overall transformation from an exposition of ideas to a drama of action is skillfully consummated, and thus ideological discussions are well integrated with the development of the plot. Perhaps most significant, Levin's choice of setting, with its Kafkaesque implications, is effective both as a structural framework for the action and as metaphor. The fortress becomes more than the locale of actual physical imprisonment. As the captives ponder metaphysical issues, it becomes apparent that their restrictions are mental as well as physical. The questions raised in the castle cannot be resolved, the actions of man and God remain unfathomable, and the thinking individual remains helpless within his moral deliberations. Unlike *Eva* or *The Fanatic,* one is made to feel the force of the human dilemma and the ultimate absurdity of the human condition in a world that man can neither comprehend nor control.

There are, nevertheless, several elements that weaken the novel. Characters are hyperbolically drawn; they tend to function more as symbols than as living personalities. Kraus is an unadulterated villain; Vered and his fellow ex-minister Remy are clearly heroic; Marianne, Remy's self-imprisoned mistress, is a romanticized portrait of the self-sacrificing female. Although Levin's ear for conversation is accurate, his descriptive language is self-consciously and overly metaphorical: "The Baron watched, even with a slight emanation of encouragement, like a surgeon watching a patient's first postoperative efforts to rise from bed" (23–24).

Perhaps most damaging to the novel's overall flow is Levin's inadequate handling of point of view, a frequent flaw in many of his works. The narrative suffers from the devisive technique of rapid and unprepared shifts in inner perspective. The story begins, for example, from Kraus's point of view. His inner thoughts are conveyed, and we begin to understand that the story is being told from the point of view of his Nazi mentality. Suddenly and unexpectedly, the reader finds himself viewing the action from the inner perspective of the aged and sensitive Vered. Similar juxtapositions occur throughout *The Stronghold,* as Levin attempts to identify the narrative voice of the novel with each of a dozen or so characters. Although this type of sophisticated handling of point of view can be extremely effective, lending multiple insights into a single event, Levin fails to maintain the necessary narrative balance that would have enhanced rather than detracted from the novel.

Despite these shortcomings, *The Stronghold* remains a more moving interpretation of the holocaust than either *Eva* or *The Fanatic.* All three novels seek to express the ineffable horror of history, but only in *The Stronghold* does Levin's technique of reduction and limitation become an effective means of relating the enormous tragedy of the holocaust. Only in *The Stronghold* did Levin succeed in creating a suitable structure and situation to contain the unrealistic course of events he wished to translate into human terms. And finally, only in *The Stronghold* do we come to feel the destruction of human lives and of the human spirit in forceful and tragic terms.

By the time *The Stronghold* appeared in 1965, Levin had largely fallen from the attention of the literary world, and there was hardly any mention of the book in either newspapers or in the various literary journals. The *New York Times*, in fact, did not even grant the novel the benefit of a full review, choosing instead to include a report on the novel, together with several other newly published works, in its weekly column "A Reader's Report." It is difficult to determine whether this lack of enthusiasm was a result of critical insight or emanated from some other, external factors, as Levin often claimed. It is true that Levin had established a reputation in the 1950s as "litigious" and, mostly as a result of his difficulties with the Anne Frank case, had alienated many influential members of the literary establishment. More relevant was the fact that Levin's unabashed Zionism and his move to Israel was regarded by many as a particularly parochial position.

Throughout the 1950s and early 1960s intellectual Jewish authors, scholars, and critics seemed to prefer a more "liberal" universalist ideology. Although American Jewish literature enjoyed tremendous critical and popular success during this period, the subjects of religion, peoplehood, the holocaust, and Israel were not among those popularized by such writers as Saul Bellow, Bernard Malamud, Philip Roth, Bruce Jay Friedman, or even Isaac Bashevis Singer.

The decline of Levin's popular and critical support in the 1960s was probably hastened by his contentious attitude and his personal difficulties. The general disinterest that greeted the publication of *Eva, The Fanatic*, and *The Stronghold* must be understood, however, as a combination of factors: objections to Levin the individual (on both personal and political grounds), a general lack of enthusiasm for his "message," and the overall mediocrity of his achievement during this period. Although Levin was, in many respects, a successful writer, he no longer commanded the critical attention he felt he deserved.

Levin's last novel of the decade, although a total departure from his earlier fiction, did little to enhance his reputation in the eyes of his supporters and detractors alike.

Gore and Igor

After the rather grim subject matter of the holocaust novels, Levin turned in a strange spirit of release to an absurd and licentious parody of the popular culture of the 1960s. *Gore and Igor* (1968), a most unusual work for an author who heretofore had produced a rather serious, often sententious, body of work, is essentially a picaresque comedy. Its dual heroes are the contemporary equivalents of the "picaro," or rascal who succeeds more through his wits than his industry. Episodic in nature, *Gore and Igor* is mostly structureless. The narrative consists of little more than a series of incidents loosely held together with little logical arrangement and with no apparent causal relationship.

There is no real plot, although the story is not without numerous twists and convolutions. Through the antics of these two picaros, and by virtue of their association with people from various societies and stations in life, Levin is able to poke fun at many of the attitudes and conventions of the 1960s. The novel, however, is not high satire. Although Levin seeks to transcend the pandemonium of the situations he creates, the ridiculous nature of his characters implies pure farce rather than any lasting political or social criticism.

Romantic in the sense of being a story of love, sex, adventure, and war, *Gore and Igor* is nevertheless strongly marked by realistic methods, not only in its frankness of language but also in its attention to quotidian detail and its emphasis on contemporary social situations—protest marches, freeways, drive-in restaurants, etc. There is an underlying pessimism to Levin's mirth, for Gore and Igor inhabit a world devoid of beauty and meaning, a fact which helps account for their extreme responses to their situations. Igor's Russia is characterized by the frozen wasteland of Siberia, work details, and political and literary repression. Gore's California is equally dismal: a world of superhighways, neon signs, junk yards, and fast-food restaurants. The novel's opening paragraph, for example, functions both as parody and metaphor: "Where the ten-lane north-south figure-eights with the east-west superparkway, a four-lane feeder zooms off to the Peaceful Ocean, bringing Bingo Beach within thirty-five minutes of the city of Angels. . . . At the very entrance to Bingo Beach, opposite Muchacha's Discount Drive-In with its array of Mexican straw furniture, stands an heroic junk pile gateway, made of stripped-down auto frames, adorned with smashed fenders in all colors like flying banners, and jeweled with polished wheel discs."[5]

The world that Levin describes—whether California, Tel Aviv, or Moscow—is overpopulated and spiritually undernourished: a conglomeration of machines, greedy individuals, and meaningless social conformity. If Gore and Igor are merely cardboard characters (which for the most part they are), they are perfectly placed in a cardboard world, their mindlessness well suited to the irrationality of their existence. In this sense, *Gore and Igor* is Levin's contribution to pop art—a means of representing the gap between conventional experience and the anarchy of existence.

The novel juxtaposes the experiences of the two heroes of the title: Gore Taylor (née Isadore Schneider), California folk singer and peace demonstrator; and Igor Dmitri Mikhailovitch, Russian "poet of the people" and well known Moscow dissident. Gore is a stereotype of the 1960s beatnik and protest poet: "Why should we shoot off all that stuff / Starvation is killing folks fast enough" (29). He is, of course, the despair of a good Jewish father ("Happy Joe," trader in junk metal and wrecked cars). "The boychick grows up," Joe laments, "scrap doesn't interest him, law, medicine, accounting, engineering either, what is he going to become, a loafer? Gore the gornisht. Now plunking a guitar" (14). But Gore does not stay around long enough to cause his father further anguish. Instead, he is off protesting the war in the middle of a Los Angeles freeway. Before the rally is over, Gore is charged with obscenity for singing his latest song: "Johnny, throw away your gun / Nature already gave you one!" (28). Eluding the vengeful and overzealous California police, Gore slips across the border into Mexico with his girl friend, Miriam Christ.

Miriam, a beautiful half-black, half-Jewish Ph.D., is a fanatic follower of the teachings of Wilhelm Reich and a believer in the great powers of orgone energy for such diverse uses as sexual stimulation, automobile fuel, and even rainmaking: "As Miriam already knew, the culminating discoveries of Dr. Wilhelm Reich, found recorded in his confidential papers after his death—to America's eternal shame, in a prison cell—were connected with the limitless application of orgone energy in all areas. Among the papers were plans for a motor, to be driven purely on orgone energy. Even more fully developed were the master's plans for orgonotic precipitation of rainfall" (74). Instead of lingering with Gore in Tijuana, Miriam sets off with a group of more scientifically disposed partners to the arid desert of the Negev where conditions are said to be ideal for orgone rain experiments.

In the meantime, oceans away, Igor is running into difficulties with the Soviet authorities. Igor, whose character appears to be roughly patterned after the poet Yevgeny Yevtushenko, is off on a world tour of concert halls, romantic interludes, and occasional flight from the more conservative elements of the Russian literary and political power structure. Eventually Igor runs into serious difficulty with the OGPU when he composes a poem protesting the arrest of a good friend and mentor who has written an anti-Soviet satire. To escape forced repatriation, Igor flees to Israel where he meets his American counterpart, Gore. Together they find refuge in the land of Zion, sharing a series of outrageous and licentious adventures which culminate, somewhat inappropriately, in the Six-Day War.

Part 1, "A Conjunction of Poets," follows the separate careers of the novel's two heroes prior to their arrival in Israel. The action shifts rapidly from one continent to the next as we follow first Gore then Igor. While Gore is involved with Miriam, Igor is having similar romantic complications, although with different results. On one of his many "cultural missions," Igor, who is known as much for his amorous prowess as for his poetry, forms a passionate liaison with the French actress Mimette, the archetypal movie star and sex-goddess: "French women are the best and Mimette is the best of the best." She, in her turn, develops a seemingly insatiable lust for Igor and manages to pursue him in his exile to Israel.

Although part 2 is entitled "Passage to Israel," it takes place after all the previously introduced characters have arrived in the Promised Land. Gore, not unlike Alexander Portnoy, tries unsuccessfully to win the favors of a healthy but reluctant Sabra. Igor encounters his old truck driving buddy from Siberia, Yashka, and his rather insipid wife, Ahuva. Yashka, a Russian Jew, many years earlier had fled the Soviet Union to establish a new life in Israel. Igor spends a good deal of time with his old friend and his wife who, as it turns out, is susceptible to Igor's amorous advances.

(Ahuva is, coincidentally, one of Dr. Miriam Christ's subjects in her latest orgone and sexual response experiments.) Gore and Igor finally come together in a violent confrontation at the café of the infamous Chava—an Israeli widow, former terrorist, and another woman of great sexual appetite. It seems that Igor is only capable of poetic creation when his libido is properly satisfied: "There was no literary emanation without copulation." The action, once Gore and Igor join forces and pool their talents, is continuous, although mostly pointless, and involves unremitting fornication, Reichian orgone boxes, frequent hair-raising truck races along the Dead Sea road, and some—although not much—writing of poetry.

Part 3, "Pen in the Pen or Equal Dungeons for All," is more of the same: peace demonstrations (Gore tries to bring peace to the Middle East through an organization known as the "Israel Arab-Jewish League for Peace and Friendship"), Miriam Christ's experiments with rainmaking devices in the Negev, and Mimette's conversion to Judaism and her relentless pursuit of Igor. The section closes with a wild truck race that leaves both Gore and Igor in the hospital and eventually, both on stretchers, on their way back to their respective countries. Gore has decided to stand trial as a protest against censorship: " 'Man, I gotta make that scene. You dig?' " Igor has opted for an equally heroic stance: he will return to Moscow in order to once again speak for the freedom of the Soviet people: " 'I will go home . . . I will speak' " (246). There is, of course, a slight mix-up at the airport: hospital charts are mysteriously switched; Gore flies off to Moscow, and Igor winds up in the United States.

The novel should have ended on this note, for the last section appears to be an afterthought. Part 4, "When Messiah Comes," is devoted to the Six-Day War with some vague references to the coming of the savior. The section, with its mostly serious tone and the relatively minor role of the novel's two heroes, appears largely out of place. Before *Gore and Igor* is over, several conclusions about the war, the arrival of the messiah, and the future of Judaism are made. These fail to ring true, however, in a novel that has concentrated so completely on the comic and the absurd. The book ends with a reference to brotherhood and future peace: "The ancient walls of Jerusalem resounded with joy, the Tower of King David shivered with happiness, and it was long before the ecstatic multitude could be quieted enough for Gore and Igor to sing in unison, in Arabic, Hebrew, Russian, and English, The Biblical lines, 'How pleasant and how good to see / Brethren dwelling in unity.' Indeed it was as though Messiah had come" (314–15).

Gore (who should not be confused with Bob Dylan, née Robert Zimmerman), Igor, Mimette, Miriam, and a host of minor characters are obvious caricatures of various figures from the popular culture of the 1960s. In *Gore and Igor*, Levin was able to seize certain qualities of each and, through exaggeration and distortion produce a burlesque, ridiculous effect. Although many of the characters and character "types" are immediately recognizable, there are no realistic figures in the novel—all are cardboard creations. Levin manipulates these creations into the most impossible situations in order to make fun of them and the conventions and institutions they represent. Few contemporary stereotypes are ignored: the protest singer, the Russian dissident, the aging movie queen, the tireless sex researcher, Israeli freedom fighters, and even Hadassah tourist ladies. *Gore and Igor* also manages to touch all the topical bases: the American peace movement, the generation gap, Zionism, the U.J.A., the Russian political-literary establishment, censorship, pornography, and Arab-Israeli relations, to name only a few. The novel has many humorous moments, for Levin's satiric barbs often hit the mark. When Igor finds himself in an Israeli police station, for instance, he notices a bust of Moses with the inscription: "Donated by Mrs. Shirley Edelstyne, Miami Beach, Florida." Even the iron door of the prison has been "Donated by the Brooklyn Law Society in memory of Judge Simon Lefkowitz." Levin's observation on sexuality in the Soviet Union is equally irreverent: "To his surprise and amusement, Igor even on his first cultural tour abroad had discovered that foreigners had a fixed idea about sex in the Soviet

Union. They were convinced that this was always a solemn exercise, accomplished in a direct, healthful, and comradely manner, without frills. Soviet women were serious, and lovemaking was a reward for good tractor-driving. . . . Apparently none of them had ever read Gorky's autobiography" (55–56).

Obviously, Levin had long been harboring a sense of humor. Written in the 1960s, much of the satire now appears dated, for the novel's emphasis is on the particular rather than the universal. *Gore and Igor* does not contain the type of lasting observations on man and society as does, for instance, Joseph Heller's *Catch 22* or Kurt Vonnegut's *Slaughterhouse-Five.* One is vaguely aware of the social and political implications behind Levin's comic vision, but they are rarely sustained enough to give his farce any meaning beyond the literal.

Nor does the novel succeed totally on the literal level—the level of pure farce. To begin with, Levin's humor is often forced; it does not spring spontaneously from his view of existence, but rather from a deliberate attempt to demonstrate his ability to keep up with the latest trends. Four letter words, for example, had, by 1968, long since lost their value to shock. Nevertheless, Levin's vulgarity and recounting of sexual exploits is endless and appears mostly gratuitous, employed more as proof of his "modernity" than for any inherent purpose. Indeed, the advance publicity by Simon and Schuster emphasized that *Gore and Igor* was "perhaps the answer to those who pictured him [Levin] as a writer of the old school"; and that now Levin had "shown the younger crop of writers that he could leap right in front of the far-out."[6]

As a result much of the humor lacks authenticity; gags fall flat, and comic sequences degenerate into slapstick sketches. Gore and Igor compete for the favors of local girls, exchange protest poems, and race across the sands of the desert. These skirmishes are meant to represent the larger confrontation between the free world and the Soviets, but these "symbolic" contests adhere more to adolescent fantasy than political metaphor: " 'What the hell!' roared Igor at Gore, 'you want an accident!' 'Naw,' yelled Gore at Igor, 'I like to see the road, not just your truck-ass,' Igor laughed and gunned his machine. 'Here goes the cosmonaut!' he shouted, even achieving a chauvinistic back-fart from his exhaust. 'First on the moon!' retorted Gore the American, shooting forward with equal speed" (183).

Gore and Igor is nevertheless an interesting experiment—Levin's attempt to chart previously unknown literary territory. His one purpose it seems was to exercise a long neglected sense of the absurd and the ridiculous. Unfortunately, the novel is mostly self-indulgent, for Levin takes full license with his story, his characters, and his plot. The novel suffers from a too loose structure, satire that is mostly limited and unsustained, and a last section that is entirely unintegrated into the whole.

Levin had always taken himself and his literary vocation seriously; his works frequently contain a "message." His novels are usually long and solemn affairs, with little or no comic relief to help lighten the load. *Gore and Igor* demonstrated that there was a humorous side to the author, that Levin was capable, at least momentarily, of relinquishing the totally serious side of his nature. There is no other example in his long opus of this ability to laugh at the more ridiculous aspect of man's existence. One wishes, of course, that he had been able to give vent to his comic vision long before, that it could have been integrated into some of his better, but overly sententious works. One wishes too, that the experiment of *Gore and Igor* was merely a prelude to a future, more finely tuned satire of war and humankind.

Unfortunately, Levin's ability to poke fun at man's foibles left him as quickly as it had arrived. After *Gore and Igor* he began work on a project that held great import for him and which was undertaken with great seriousness. For years he had been gathering material for a historical novel of the early years of Palestine. It was to take almost four years to write (after years of planning), and in many ways it lived up to his expectations. *The Settlers* represents the culmination of Levin's total involvement with Judaism and Jewish history. But the novel contains no hint of the author of *Gore and Igor*, no mild reminder of the writer who was able to laugh at the world around him. That man it seems existed only for a very short time and in a very limited context.

Chapter Six
The Committed Zionist

By 1970, Levin, no longer plagued by feelings of dual loyalties, was comfortable and secure in his role as a writer of Jewish themes. Shunning the label "American Jewish writer" assumed by many of his contemporaries, Levin believed his work to be specifically and uniquely "Jewish": "Saul Bellow and Philip Roth, two of our most famous American Jewish writers, have made it very clear in the last few years that they consider themselves to be writers who are American Jews who write about Jews because that happens to be the material of their lives. But they don't consider themselves to be distinctly Jewish writers. They don't want to be limited. On the contrary, I feel that I am a Jewish writer."[1] For Levin, the label "Jewish" implied neither limitation nor negation, but an ability to see the Jewish people as a distinct quality in world life. Levin's desire to write of Jewish subjects led to his interest in the particular aspects of the Jewish past, its present, and its future. Consonant with this interest was an intense concern with the life and security of the state of Israel. Levin's fiction in the 1970s—specifically *The Settlers* and its sequel, *The Harvest* —reflect this commitment to Jewish identity and the survival of a Jewish homeland.

The Settlers

Levin always demonstrated a strong preference for fiction that was close to fact. *The Old Bunch* described what happened to a group of Levin's contemporaries in Chicago during the 1920s and early 1930s. *Citizens*, reportorial in style and its use of detail, told the story of ten steel strikers shot and killed by the Chicago police in 1937. *Compulsion*, although more psychological than historical, was based on the facts surrounding the famous Leopold and Loeb case. *Eva, The Fanatic*, and *The Stronghold* document, in part, the massacre of European Jews by the Nazis. *The Settlers* (1972), like these earlier efforts, is concerned with history and the relationship between historical events and human lives.

Like *Yehuda*, Levin's first Zionist novel, *The Settlers* is set in the early days of Palestine and seeks to recreate the mood and atmosphere of the years prior to the foundation of the state of Israel. From the time of the publication of *Yehuda* in 1931, Levin began to envision a more comprehensive and more ambitious novel of the settlement of Palestine: "I first planned the book in 1934," Levin recalled in a 1972 interview, "I even gave a few pages of outline to a publisher." For several reasons the book did not get written then. One was financial; another was psychological: "I felt the book should be done by someone who had lived it more." The idea, dormant for many years, surfaced several decades later: "I finally got to an age where I realized if I don't do it now I never will. The material inside me was pressing for expression."[2]

Technique. *The Settlers* conforms to the literary conventions associated with the genre of the historical novel; it is a hybrid combination of history and fiction, aimed at evoking the spirit of an age as well as actual events. Although *The Settlers* is a deliberate response to a specific history, Levin's concerns are not those of the historian. As a novelist, he is not so much interested in determining the subtle political causes of events, as in portraying individuals and their responses to those events. The novel's focus is on the settlers themselves: farmers, tractor drivers, night watchmen, soldiers, mothers, children, and kibbutz workers; rather than on political or military leaders. Thus the device of the historical novel offered Levin a means of recording the history of the settlement of Palestine; at the same time it allowed him the novelist's freedom to present a story of human lives—of love and sorrow, of triumph and defeat.

The story of the history of Israel is told as the story of a single family, their flight from Russia during the pogroms, and their struggle to establish a new life in a barren and hostile land. The saga of the fictional Chaimovitch family, whose name derives from the Hebrew word for life, *chaim*, is based on the actual experiences of the family of Yitzhak Chicik, whom Levin had met many years earlier in Chicago and to whom the book is dedicated. "He was a Palestinian who came to the University of Chicago in 1928 and I was a newspaper man whom he tried to teach Hebrew. I didn't learn much Hebrew because I wanted to know about him and his family."[3] Chicik filled Levin's head with stories about his family's flight from Russia and their life as early pioneers along the Jordan River. Almost forty years later, Levin used the Chiciks as models for the Chaimovitch family.

Like the Chiciks, the Chaimovitch clan was large: nine children in all. Together they formed a small community. Levin used the group, in much the same way as he did the bunch in *The Old Bunch*, to examine a wide range of humanity. The movement of the novel, like that of his earlier work, is centripetal: each of the sons and daughters moves outward to experience life in a new land. The cynosure around which all the activity moves is always the central family unit and their small farm in Galilee. Because the family is so large (by the end of the novel it is extended to include several spouses and grandchildren), Levin is able to describe the diverse segments of the growing population of the new country: young and old, immigrant and "sabra," male and female. The novel's narrative moves from one Chaimovitch to another in order to record various experiences through the different generations. "They came as an entire family," Levin explained, "the older people as well as the young. . . . This gave me a wider range to work in, a bigger canvas. I had, for example, the effort of the older people to adjust. And I had the generation gap which existed even then. The father and mother were very orthodox; the sons and daughters were already free thinkers."[4]

Although the members of the Chaimovitch family are based on those of the Chicik family, they also have their genesis in the Old Testament and thus function on the symbolic level as well as the literal. Specifically, *The Settlers* has its roots in the biblical story of the patriarch Jacob and the settlement of his numerous offspring into the land. The elder Chaimovitch, for instance, Yankel (Yiddish for Jacob), is the archetypal father of a clan that is both rebellious and loving. His first born son, like that of Jacob's biblical son, is named Reuven; the second, Gidon—or Gideon—is, like his namesake, a soldier. Yankel's eldest daughter Leah (Jacob's wife in the Bible), a large, powerful yet tender woman, becomes, like the biblical Leah, the figurative—if not literal—wellspring of a people. Shulamith, the most beautiful and the most feminine of the Chaimovitch daughters, is reminiscent in both name and character of the seductive dancer portrayed in Solomon's "Song of Songs." Each member of the family therefore becomes allegorical, a personification of the various types of Jews who came to settle a new land.

Theme and characters. *The Settlers* is the story of the Chaimovitch family and their emigration from Russia to Palestine shortly after the abortive 1905 revolution. Pogroms, stifling ghettos, economic restrictions, and widespread anti-Semitism were common throughout Eastern Europe at the beginning of the century and resulted in the mass flight of Jews from the continent. While the majority emigrated to America, a smaller but determined segment went to Palestine, then under Turkish rule. These Eastern European Jews were a part of the socialist-Zionist movement, followers of Theodore Herzl, who preached a return of the Jews to the promised land.

The first part of the novel, "Return," traces the route of those who chose to escape the pogroms of the Czar and emphasizes the difficulties of settlement. Curiously, Levin shuns the use of dates throughout the book, and the reader must depend on familiar events such as the Russian Revolution and the start of World War I as landmarks. The book begins in 1907; the Chaimovitches are on board a ship bound for Jaffa with six of their eight living children (one has died in infancy; the two eldest have gone on ahead; another will be born in Palestine). The opening image is one of familial closeness and motherly protection, as Feigel Chaimovitch draws her young sons and daughters lovingly around her: "Under God's stars, with the younger children lying close on one side and the other side of her, the girls curled against each other on the left and the boys on her right, Feigel truly felt herself like a great mother bird with her brood nestling under her wings."[5]

Yankel and Feigel have left Russia at the urging of their oldest son Reuven who, together with his sister Leah, has already spent a year in Palestine. Reuven and Leah were part of a group of young Zionist pioneers who founded the first "kvutsa," or labor cooperative, forerunner of the modern kibbutz. Imbued with the socialist ideal and stimulated by Herzl's messianic vision of a Jewish state, Reuven and Leah send back enthusiastic reports about the prospects of the country and the possibilities that awaited new settlers. Although their year has been filled with hardship and disappointment, their love for the land and devotion to their ideal has remained as strong as the day they first set eyes on the desert spot that was to become their new home: "This was a moment that neither was to forget. . . . The skinlike smoothness of the untrodden sand, the absolute cleanliness of all creation, the pure sea-blue of the quiet Mediterranean, the solitude around them and the presence of each other exalted them. We have done it! Brother! Sister! We are here! Leah's and Reuven's eyes said this to each other in a pledge of fervor, joy, dedication, a declaration that what they had known in their souls to be their true course was indeed so" (46).

The Settlers, however, does not project an unrealistic utopian vision of the promised land, for the novel fully explores the harsh realities of the pioneer experience and the clash between the settler's dream of a new life and the actuality encountered. While on board ship, for example, Yankel dreams of an idyllic new life: "A place of dignity, among lemon trees, a barn with a good cow or two, a goat, green fields, and going out with his sons to their labors. Sabbath at ease beneath his own fig and vine"

(38). His first glimpse of Palestine, however, is the port city of Jaffa, and the reality of the crowded dirty city overwhelms him: "Moment by moment Yankel's heart was growing heavier with misgivings. Now the stench and filth of the Oriental city was upon him. This was not what he had envisioned. . . . In the swarming passageway they had to string out single file. The stink was in the very stones—urine, garbage, dead fish. Fierce, ugly cats darted from behind the stalls. And the Arab children, some entirely naked, the older ones in a few rags, pressed around them crying 'baksheesh.' Tots hardly bigger than Avramchick, beggars already! Other children sat apathetic against the hovels, their eyes crowded with flies" (37–38).

Within a few days the Chaimovitches leave the unpleasant city of Jaffa to settle on a small piece of desert land in Mishkan Yaakov on the bank of the Jordan River, not far from Tiberius. But even here there are problems: the land is parched and rocky, ruled by despotic Turks, dominated by hostile Arabs, and ravaged by disease. Again Yankel's disappointment and frustration well up in him, as he rages against his eldest son whom he blames for bringing them to a "wilderness of murderous Arabs." Nevertheless, Yankel gradually begins to accept the reality of his new life, not because he believes in the socialist ideal, but because his faith in the homeland is based on deeply held religious convictions. "We must restore ourselves to our land," Yankel ultimately concludes, "we must bind ourselves to the soil" (902).

Yankel is not, of course, the only member of the family who has difficulty adjusting to a new way of life. As the narrative moves from one character to the next, we begin to see the unique difficulties faced by each Chaimovitch. Feigel, for instance, fears for her children and for the unity of the family group, especially in the face of the new labor cooperatives. Leah's story dominates much of the book, and in many ways she is the central figure. She is larger and stronger than most men and must continually struggle to maintain her own sense of feminity: "She had grown like some Russian peasant woman, broad-boned, tall, . . . taller than her brother Reuven, full-bodied, with great red cheeks and strong teeth" (19). With her devotion to the settler's cause, her simple goodness, and her capacity for hard work, she is of great use to the community. But she ultimately remains a somewhat tragic figure, deserted by her lover and unable to find a husband. Reuven, by contrast, is slight, sickly, and subject to attacks of malaria. Moreover, he is often frustrated by the force of his own idealism—impatient and intolerant of an existence that does not conform to his utopian vision. Dvora and Eliza, the next oldest daughters, suffer the consequences of a people continually at war. Dvora's fiancé is shot down on their wedding day while guarding the fields of the settlement against Arab attack. Her sister Eliza (who changes her name to Shulamith), the most vain and most beautiful of the Chaimovitch girls, has a tragic love affair with a German aviator which nearly destroys her and her relationship with her family.

In many ways the most interesting of the Chaimovitch children is Gidon, Reuven's younger brother who comes of age in Palestine. Old enough to remember with fondness his former life in Russia, Gidon is psychologically caught between the new world of his brother and the old world of his father. Unlike his brother, he cannot embrace atheism or the ideals of socialism. Yet, watching his father recite his morning prayers, Gidon is aware of his estrangement from traditional Judaism and from the customs of his father: "Now his father touched his lips to the tallis and, with the old circular movement that Gidon had never quite caught, swung himself into the prayer shawl as he swung it about him, so that he was wrapped away in the world beyond. Thus from childhood he had always seemed to Gidon . . . removed from them" (23–24). But Gidon is also aware of his unique identity as a Jew and the importance of his past and his God. "I am a Jew," he reminds himself, "a Jew bound in with my God." And it is this sense of historical continuity that strikes Gidon and causes his elation on the morning of his arrival in the new land: "Somehow in this arrival Gidon found himself listening, harkening to the words he automatically recited in the prayer, his own words as they came from his lips today, and the same words from his father. Today it did not seem . . . meaningless and foolish to repeat by rote the same words of prayer each morning" (25).

Taken as a unit, the Chaimovitches form the nucleus of the novel. A host of satellite characters, however, revolve around them and help demonstrate Levin's motif of settlement. There is, for example, Zev the Hotblood, the "shomer," or watchman, whose proclivity toward violence endangers the whole community; Sara Aaronson, who eventually becomes a spy for the British in World War I; Handsome Moshe—a womanizer, and the only man Leah has ever loved—who returns to Russia in order to work for the revolution; and the one-armed Russian soldier-hero, Josef Trumpeldor (one of the many historical figures in the novel), who tries to persuade the British to create a Jewish army to help reconquer the Jewish homeland.

Although many of these personalities are interesting, none are multidimensional, for *The Settlers* is not a novel of characterization. As in *The Old Bunch*, Levin sacrifices psychological depth to the portrayal of a wide panorama of events and action. Something is always happening: Dvora finds a new love and eventually marries; Feigel bears her last child; Reuven is conscripted into the service of the Turks and journeys to Damascus; there are festivals and celebrations, as well as hostilities and retaliations. Within this vast tableau there is little opportunity for the full development of individualized personalities. Although the members of the Chaimovitch family are sufficiently vivid to remain clearly in the reader's mind, they exist more as representative types—personifications of particular aspects or problems of settlement life—than as complex, idiosyncratic characters.

The emphasis on the generic rather than the specific continues in the second part of the novel. Book 2, "Choice," which is longer and less unified than the first, embraces the entire period and much of the action of World War I. Here the stage broadens and members of the family are scattered as far away as England, Russia, and Turkey.

When the war breaks out the entire Jewish community is thrown into confusion. Which country, for example, should the Chaimovitch family back? Russia, their native land? Turkey, the rulers of the place they now occupy? Or the British, who promise to rout the Turks and thus free Palestine from Ottoman tyranny? Some of the young men, like Reuven, are forced into the employ of the Turks. Others, like Gidon, convinced that a British victory will result in a free Jewish state, enlist in the British army. With Josef Trumpeldor as their leader, they set off for England in the hope that the government there will establish a Jewish army to fight beside the British forces. Such an unorthodox concept, however, is beyond the thinking of the high command. Gidon and his compatriots are assigned instead to the muleteers (the "Zion Mule Brigade," as they are called). Disappointed and bitter, they nevertheless conduct themselves with dignity. At the battle of Gallipoli, the brigade demonstrates such heroism in the performance of their humble duties that they are eventually allowed to take part in the liberation of Jerusalem.

The capture of the ancient city is the climax of the novel, culminating most of the action of book 2. But here too, the clash between dream and reality is evident. Although liberation occurs on the eve of Chanukah, and although the event is heralded as the first step in returning the land to the Jews, the celebration is portrayed, ironically, in Christian terms: "All the church-bells in England, in France, in Rome rang out the victory, *Jerusalem. Jerusalem.* In Notre Dame special services were held: it was as though the Crusades had triumphed again, the Holy City was restored to Christendom, . . . as a divine gift, for Christmas" (754). The Jews once again find themselves superfluous, strangers in the city they had hoped would be their home: ". . . white-robed priests, and black-robed priests, . . . and the bishops, and the Greek and Armenian and Russian popes with broad sashes and bejeweled crosses and silver and gold embroidery, all assembled in the square by the Tower of David. . . . The Christians had returned as in the days of the Crusades, and driven out the

Moslem rulers from the City of David" (757–58). Again, the Jews are made to feel the tragic irony of the diaspora. As one of the pioneers wryly observes: "It was not as though the bridegroom had arrived to find the bride missing, . . . it was simply as though the Jews were at the wrong wedding" (757). Ironically, life under the British will not prove to be radically different from that of the previous rulers. As the novel closes, we are shown the beginnings of British governance: harsh, intolerant, and insensitive to the problems and needs of the Jewish people.

Although the liberation of Jerusalem is the dramatic conclusion of the novel, there are subsequent family adventures to be recorded. Reuven returns from Damascus with a wife; Leah, however, remains single, somewhat satisfied for the time being as the leader of a young girls' farm settlement. Gidon, released from the army, eventually marries the daughter of a Hebrew teacher in Jerusalem. And Mati, the youngest Chaimovitch, the "one born in Eretz," is sent, against Yankel's wishes, to study at the Herzl Gymnasia in Tel Aviv. Yankel, alone and defeated, feels himself slipping into the oblivion and neglect of old age: "My beliefs my sons don't follow and our God you don't worship" (901). As the novel closes, Yankel muses over his fate and begins to perceive the parallel between his life and that of his biblical namesake. Like the patriarch Jacob, Yankel has seen his family torn by strife, pestilence, and war. Yet, recalls Yankel, the family of Jacob survived to settle the land and a nation. So, Yankel hopes, it will be with his family; perhaps even that to which he objects will be "for the good": "Yankel gave the boy a shoulder-hug and said, 'Go with my blessing.' . . . A saying from the ancient sage, the one called Gamzu, came to Yankel. It was the very saying from which the sage got his name, meaning, 'this too.' For to everything, even every disaster, the sage was wont to respond, 'Gam zu l'tovah'—This too is for the good" (904).

Conclusion. *The Settlers* is an optimistic novel; the Chaimovitch story is one of triumph over the weight of historical determinism. Yet Levin's treatment of the theme of settlement is a perceptive blend of realism and irony. His characters are devoted Zionists, but they are not saintly. His Jewish pioneers are seen realistically: often petty, quarrelsome, obstinate, and silly. Levin's interpretation of the Zionist motif itself is equally objective, destroying as it does the peurile and romantic image often portrayed in American films and popular novels of the birth of Israel. The main theme of *The Settlers*—the clash between dream and reality—lends force and credence to Levin's final hope for the future.

As fiction portraying historical events, the novel has both strengths and weaknesses. The beauty of *The Settlers* lies in its variety and in its vivid depiction of the past. Although the panorama is wide, stretching as it does from Palestine to Russia and from England to Damascus, Levin manages to control his material in such a way as not to detract from the emotional center of the story. Documentary material is handled intelligently and without manipulation; fictional characters and events are cleverly integrated with historical ones to give the reader the feel of history as well as the drama of individual lives.

The Settlers succeeds best as historical fiction, as a novel that recreates the spirit of an age and shows how that spirit was reflected in a particular place and time. As such, *The Settlers* awakens our imagination to a lively sense of the past. The story of the Chaimovitch family is told in such a way that it not only becomes part of the grand pattern of historical events, but also functions as a microcosm of the survival of an entire people. Each of the sons and daughters takes part in some small way in the founding of a nation. Political events touch the family members personally, and thus the reader experiences the great sweep of history on the one hand and everyday reality on the other. Levin deals with the lives of ordinary men and women: the Chaimovitches produce no great statesmen or generals. But each character represents some human element that is essential to nation building: Reuven's idealism, Yankel's stoicism, Leah's strength, and Feigel's devotion. Collectively and individually, they give meaning and resonance to the novel's historic purpose.

There are, of course, several elements that weaken the novel. Most significantly, the book is too long; had it been shorter, its impact would have been greater. Levin was never a writer of economy, and *The Settlers* unfortunately suffers from the same flaw that marked much of his earlier work. Levin is well steeped in the history of Palestine; but his desire to recount all the details of the nation's early history, rather than the salient or representative features of the period, causes the novel to sprawl unnecessarily. Like a good historian, Levin attempts to recreate an entire era with a huge cast of characters and a multitude of incidents. As a novelist, however, he fails to select those details that function allegorically, that project a larger significance. As the novel stands (almost 850 pages in the hardbound edition, over 900 pages in paperback), there is little relationship between the novel's theme and its loose internal structure.

There are other problems as well. Levin's narrative technique, for instance, seems inappropriate for his long family saga. *The Settlers* contains no unifying point of view, no central figure with whom the reader can identify from beginning to end. The narrative "eye" shifts constantly from one Chaimovitch to another, and even from the family to the various members of the community. Like Levin's earlier communal novel, *The Old Bunch*, the point of view is collective rather than personal. But whereas this diffusion of narrative consciousness was an effective means of conveying the collective experience of the bunch, it is not well suited for the historical perspective of *The Settlers.* Inappropriate, too, is Levin's own need to identify with each of the many characters. The author of *The Settlers* is not detached from his story; he does not stand aside as an omniscient observer as one would expect. Instead, Levin has chosen to identify closely with all his characters, describing the inner thoughts and emotions of each. The reader does not benefit from this type of multiple perspective, for it is not possible to enter the inner lives of so many personalities, not all of whom are interesting or significant.

There is also a related problem of language: the text is cluttered with Yiddish, Hebrew, and even some Arabic words and phrases that are not explained in a glossary. (In the subsequent paperback edition Levin did include a list of almost 150 words and their definitions.) The meaning of these words is rarely clear within the text itself; as a result, the narrative flow (for those unfamiliar with Hebrew and Yiddish) is often interrupted. Moreover, Levin's efforts to imbue the language of his pioneers with mythic qualities appears equally contrived: "And he would go forth and lead the Jews to Eretz. He would go forth, Manahem, into the homeland." Such attempts, which occur throughout the novel, to imitate the tone and rhythm of the Bible conflict with Levin's attempt to portray the everyday reality of settlement life.

This is not to say, however, that *The Settlers* fails to accomplish its purpose, which is the dramatic telling of the story of the return of the Jews to the biblical land. In spite of its weaknesses, the novel succeeds in recreating both the history of the settlement of Israel and the forces and emotions which motivated that settlement. More significantly, *The Settlers* dramatically demonstrates the will toward Jewish survival and the continuity of a people who refused to succumb to the powerful forces of history.

Levin took longer to write *The Settlers* than usual—almost four years in the actual composition as well as years in the planning. Coming after the absurd and mostly pointless comedy of *Gore and Igor*, *The Settlers* represented a serious and purposeful effort. The book was published by Simon and Schuster in 1972. By most standards, the novel was a popular success: it was on and off the best-seller lists for several months, selling in excess of 50,000 hardcover copies.[6] It was a special choice of the Book of the Month Club, had good sales in England, and has been translated into more than a dozen languages.

Nevertheless, Levin again felt a sense of ostracism, of being ignored by the New York "literary mafia": "With *The Settlers* I was to find myself mysteriously virtually blacklisted in the New York area."[7] Correctly or not, Levin claimed that the novel was "blacked out" in New York City because the subject matter was "too Jewish." Granville Hicks did review the novel for the *New York Times Book Review* (23 April 1972), but there was no mention of the book in the daily book review column, nor in the national magazines (*Time, Newsweek, Saturday Review*, etc.). Reviewers outside New York were generally more receptive to the novel than critics from either the *Times* or the *Post*. Granville Hicks (Levin objected to the choice of reviewer referring to him as "the guru of the proletarian school") did call the novel Levin's "most ambitious" work and "in all likelihood" his best treatment of this particular subject but then went on to criticize Levin's portrayal of historic events as too diffuse. Similarly, John Barkham, writing for the *New York Post* (2 May 1972), referred to *The Settlers* as Levin's "new and ambitious novel," but found fault with the book's length, language, and characterization. Whereas the *Chicago Sun-Times* (7 May 1972) was unqualified in its praise, calling the novel "a huge panoramic saga, Tolstoyan in scope . . . surely the *War and Peace* of all books ever written about Israel." And the *Los Angeles Times* (7 May 1972) called Levin "a gifted writer" and *The Settlers* a "massive and convincing account of the early days of the settlement of Palestine."

None of this, of course, either proves or disproves Levin's claims of victimization. It is true that the concept of Jewish nationalism was not intellectually in vogue among Jewish writers and intellectuals in the late 1960s and early 1970s. It is very possible that for this reason *The Settlers* was viewed by many as provincial or chauvinistic in its outlook and limited in its subject and theme. Nevertheless, it is doubtful that any group willfully conspired against Levin in any systematic way. In truth, Levin was mostly a forgotten writer by 1972. His last succcessful novel (certainly his last well-known work) was *Compulsion*, published eighteen years earlier. The combined sales of his two most recent works (*Gore and Igor* and *The Stronghold*) did not reach 20,000. Neither attracted any critical attention. As a result, the publication of *The Settlers* failed to stir any great interest in the literary world.

Yet *The Settlers* is without doubt one of Levin's finest achievements and deserves to be viewed as such. There are certain problems with the novel, deficiencies that occur in many of Levin's works: an overly long narrative, a confused point of view, and some minor problems with language. Nevertheless, *The Settlers* succeeds as fiction that recreates history, for the story of the Chaimovitches exists against a background of a whole civilization.

In terms of Levin's development as a writer the novel has even greater significance, for *The Settlers* represents Levin's final concept of an intrinsically Jewish literature, one with meaningful ties to Jewish history and the modern state of Israel. Far from having to disguise the Jewish identity of his characters as he did in the 1920s and 1930s, Levin now wrote from a self-consciously Jewish perspective. In his attempt to think and write like a Jew, Levin had to draw upon sources outside America—the history of Israel, for example—and to experiment with language that included Hebrew and Yiddish, as well as with biblical references and archetypes. All of this was not completely successful, but it demonstrated that Levin had finally arrived at a point in his career whereby he was able to create from the demands of his own psyche rather than those of contemporary literary tastes.

More than any previous work, *The Settlers* represents Levin's commitment to Israel and the survival of a homeland. Although Levin always expressed an intense interest in Jewish history, and although he often felt a need to express that interest in his fiction, *The Settlers* is Levin's most complete statement on Zionism and the significance of seeking one's Jewish identity in Israel. For the rest of the 1970s Levin continued to write of his renewed concern for the state of Israel—its history, its people, and its future.

The Harvest

The Harvest (1978), while an independent work published six years after *The Settlers*, forms, as Levin stated, "a novelistic pair" with his 1972 novel. Although there is no specific reference to a sequel, the inconclusive ending of *The Settlers* implies continuation. Levin had, in fact, envisioned a two-volume epic from the beginning: "I conceived the idea of a two-volume story of the people of Israel in 1934. During the years since, I have written many other things, but this story of a nation in rebirth never left my mind, so that all my observation and experience went into the making of these two books."[8]

Whereas *The Settlers* dealt with the early years of settlement, *The Harvest* treats the history of Palestine from 1927 to the foundation of the modern state of Israel in 1948. The former shares with *The Settlers* the Chaimovitch family as focal point of the history Levin wishes to convey. At the conclusion of *The Settlers*, the Chaimovitch roots—planted with great difficulty and at the cost of much suffering—appear secure, as does the Jewish claim to the land. The nation and its people have begun to grow; the Chaimovitch children are mostly married with offspring of their own. The hope for an independent state of Israel is alive in all.

In the last scene of *The Settlers*, Mati, the youngest Chaimovitch and the only one born in Palestine, is sent from his family by his brothers and sisters, against the wishes of his pious and more traditionally oriented father, to Tel Aviv to be educated. At the outset of *The Harvest* (several years later), he is boarding a ship for the United States where he hopes to continue his education at the University of Chicago. Mati is now twenty, an age that is symbolic because it corresponds exactly with the length of the Chaimovitch stay in Palestine. As Mati prepares to bid his native land farewell, Levin reminds us of the particular significance of Mati's birth: "On the old docks of Jaffa, exactly where the Chaimovitch family had arrived twenty years back—the extent of Mati's lifetime, since he was already felt in the womb during the drawn-out voyage from Odessa—they were all gathered at summer's end in 1927 to see the lad off to America."[9] Although Mati's personal drama dominates much of the narrative of *The Harvest*, Levin is more concerned with the presentation of history than the portrayal of individual personalities. *The Harvest* is not so much Mati's personal story as it is the history of a period and of the creation of a nation.

The novel is divided into four "Books," each dealing with a specific aspect of the history Levin describes. Book 1, "The Emissary," follows Mati in his voyage from Palestine to Chicago, his experiences at the university, and his romance with his future American wife. The character of Mati and much of his story is based on that of Levin's acquaintance in Chicago, Yitzhak Chicik, to whom *The Settlers* is dedicated and from whom Levin received much of his information about the early days of Palestine. "The main character," Levin later recounted, "did as the book says, study in Chicago, and I studied Hebrew with him and got to know his family intimately through long conversations."[10] As a child, Mati was precocious; as a young man he is handsome, clever, and successful. At the University of Chicago, he earns a degree in economics. More significantly, he learns to fly a plane and dreams of a future Jewish airforce.

Book 2, "The Bride," follows Mati and his new wife Dena to England where Mati finishes his education at the London School of Economics. Whereas book 1 is tightly organized around Mati's experiences (and told from his point of view), the stage broadens in book 2, and Mati's story is subsumed by larger, more universal events. Fictional characters are intermingled with historical personages. David Ben-Gurion, Moshe Dayan, Golda Meyerson (who later became Golda Meir), numerous heads of state, and world renowned figures such as Leonard Bernstein and Toscanini, to name only a few, all play roles of some significance in the narrative. In London, for example, Mati meets with David Ben-Gurion, and the two begin to institute a plan for a secret national airforce.

Eventually, Mati and Dena leave England and return to Palestine. Dena, like Mati's mother many years earlier, is pregnant upon her arrival in the homeland. Her identification with the land is immediate and deeply rooted in what appears to be a Jewish collective unconscious. Her first sight of Jerusalem "brought a shivery feeling as though you were part of some eternal ongoing" (253). And later, alone in the Jordan Valley, she experiences "the strangest reaching back, like some faint, faint signal from pre-memory . . . the mysterious sense of coming home" (267).

Book 3, "The Whirlwind," begins with the Nazi invasion of Poland. As its title suggests, book 3 is the story of the war in Europe as well as the struggle of the Palestinian Jews to achieve independence from the British. The Nazi holocaust is given even greater meaning through parallel events in Palestine: the sinking of a ship carrying illegal refugees and the subsequent drowning of thousands of European Jews, Arab attacks on Jewish villages, Jewish reprisals, and the bombing of the King David Hotel. Nevertheless, the tragedy of Europe and Hitler's extermination of millions of Jews becomes the emotional center of book 3. Throughout the course of events, the Chaimovitches are made to feel the horror of the holocaust on a personal basis. The entire Russian branch of the family is destroyed as a result of a brutal pogrom in Cherezinka. Mati's brother-in-law, Manahem, is caught by the Gestapo while on a secret mission to Nazi occupied Europe and sent to Auschwitz. Much of book 3 is devoted to the description of the atrocities of World War II: Babi Yar, Buchenwald, the bloody pogroms of the Rumanian army, mass killings in Kiev, Odessa, and Cherenzinka. Little is left out, and almost every tragic event touches the lives of one or another Chaimovitch.

Book 4, "Out of Chaos," concludes Levin's history, recounting the closing days of the war and the final struggle to establish the state of Israel. With the termination of the war in Europe, open hostilities break out in Palestine, as Jews and Arabs fight to control the uncertain future of the land. With the exit of the British, comes all-out war, then triumph for the Jews. Just as *The Settlers* culminated with World War I and the liberation of Jerusalem, *The Harvest* concludes with the end of World War II and a Jewish victory over their Arab neighbors. But as in 1917, the 1948 victory is tenuous and is achieved at enormous costs. Israel, with the help of Jews around the world, has begun to rise out of the wasteland of the desert. But the aftermath of the holocaust casts its ugly shadow over the present and the future. The implication is clear: the struggle for the life and security of the new state of Israel, as well as for the future of Judaism itself, is perpetual. The novel does not end on a hopeful note, but one of beseechment, as Mati—now the governor of Jaffa—despairingly cries out amidst still another attack on his city: "Oh God, you devil. Oh, you murderer. . . . What more can you want of us?" (670).

The Harvest suffers from many of the same weaknesses as *The Settlers*: an overly long narrative, an inability to create complex characters, and a lack of a strong narrative voice. But unlike *The Settlers, The Harvest* has few strong points to counterbalance its shortcomings. Gone, for example, is the confrontation between the new and the old Jew so movingly portrayed in *The Settlers*. The strong patriarch Yankel who, in the earlier novel, desperately struggled to hold his family together as they gradually broke away to a more secular way of life, becomes merely a vestige in *The Harvest*—a senile old man who "more and more loved to reflect and discuss with himself in solitude" (661).

The Settlers was excessively long and at times needlessly convoluted. But Levin's panoramic treatment of the grand march of history was balanced by an unromantic rendering of everyday conditions in the early settlements. The harshness of life in the desert, as well as the pain and suffering of the Chaimovitch family were presented realistically and without sentimentality. The little farm at Mishkan Yaakov always seemed precariously balanced between survival and extinction, as was the Zionist dream itself. In *The Harvest* Levin yields to the more sentimental aspects of Zionism, and his rendering of history is often simplified or romanticized. As Pearl K. Bell in her 1978 *Commentary* article points out, Levin's characters—both fictional and historical—do not respond to experience as complex human beings, but rather as impossible heroes or heroines: "Wonderful and terrible things happen to everyone in the book. . . . his characters are so insufferably fetching, noble, and loveable that they seem nothing more than Israeli fiddlers on the roof."[11]

Although *The Harvest* teaches history, it fails to delineate human nature. The novel contains none of the personal conflict evident in *The Settlers*: the clash between dream and reality, the ideological discord between Yankel and his children, or the lonely struggle of the Chaimovitches to survive in a strange land. From the beginning the land holds the settlers, but we are aware that their existence is a contingent one. They remain in Palestine because it is the ancient land of promise, and because they are bound to it by toil, sacrifice, and suffering. The microcosm of the family farm and the historical metaphor implied in the telling of the Chaimovitch story, so carefully developed in *The Settlers*, fails to function in *The Harvest.*

Whereas the narrative of *The Settlers* appears at times to be confusing, that of *The Harvest* is totally without structure. The novel has no continuous story line and no controlling narrative device. The action moves rapidly and randomly through New York, Berlin, Rome, Istanbul, Babi Yar, Jaffa, Paris, Kiev; in short, through most of Europe, Asia, America, and the Middle East. Levin's story of Israel includes such unrelated events as the stock market crash, the Leopold-Loeb murder case, and the discovery of the Dead Sea Scrolls. Political and social events are examined, but individual emotions and reactions are lost in Levin's need to convey history.

The Harvest thus succeeds more as history than as art. The events leading up to and resulting in the creation of the state of Israel are well documented, but they do not have the quality of being lived. Individuals and individual sensibilities are not important in the novel, and characters seem manipulated to suit the author's presentation of historical material.

Collectively the two novels are nevertheless an impressive mural of the fifty years that changed the course of Jewish history. They reflect Levin's sincerity as a writer of Jewish themes, his commitment to peoplehood, his intense concern for the state of Israel, and his erudite knowledge of history. Together *The Settlers* and *The Harvest* capture the deep, personal longings for a homeland, as well as the many dramatic events that resulted in the birth of a nation.

Conclusion: Levin and Israel

As early as 1955, the critic Harold Ribalow observed that Levin was one of the few American Jewish writers who "steadily saw the Jewish people whole, and thereby included Zionist themes with persistence throughout his work."[12] If this was true in the 1950s, it had greater validity in the 1970s, for Levin wrote exclusively of Israel and its people throughout the decade. But Levin's interest in Israel as literary subject began, as Ribalow states, much earlier. Exactly fifty years prior to the publication of *The Harvest*, Levin wrote "Maurie Finds His Medium," a short story in which an American Jewish hero searches for meaning and fulfillment in Palestine. Maurie, an aspiring writer, finds excuses for his failures in alienation: "I am out of place in America. . . . What right have I to scribble in this American language?"[13] After a feeble attempt to write in Yiddish, Maurie decides to seek his artistic identity in Palestine. Once there he discovers that painting is the only "language" in which he can express himself as a Jew and as an artist. Unfortunately, Maurie's art proves to be no better than his fiction: "hackneyed, common repetitions of landscapes and Arab heads, banal, except for an occasional splash of outrageously brilliant and meaningless color."[14]

There is implicit irony in Maurie's misguided search for self-expression. Yet one cannot help feel that Levin too found his medium in the 1970s and his ability to think and write like a Jew.

Throughout his career Levin wrote of the various aspects of Israel and Zionism. His first book of Palestinian life, *Yehuda* (1931), reflected an optimistic and generally positive view of settlement life and the Zionist ideal. Levin's next Israeli novel,

My Father's House (1947), projected his own deep feeling for the importance of a Jewish homeland. Levin's views on Jews and Zionism, however, are not without an understanding of the more complex issues involved. His satiric portrait of Zionist fund raising in *The Old Bunch*, for example, drew sharp criticism from the B'nai B'rith. Several years later *Commentary* published "After All I Did For Israel," an uncharacteristically funny and sardonic portrait of American Jews who devote their time and energy to Zionist causes, but who are bewildered and upset when their own children decide they want to leave the United States and devote their lives to Israel. "My own son isn't interested in our life any more," Levin's protagonist—and the community's most successful fund raiser—laments. "After all I did for Israel, this is how I get paid."[15]

Interestingly, Levin wrote another, very different story of Israel between the publication of *The Settlers* and the completion of *The Harvest*. *The Spell of Time* (1974) is a brief fantasy set in Jerusalem around the time of Israeli independence. The novella is a strange love story with elements from modern science and Hassidic mysticism. Felicité (the name, which means "happiness," recalls Flaubert's "A Simple Heart"), a beautiful, young French scientist, arrives in Jerusalem to study under Professor Uriel Buchhalter, a distinguished biochemist. The professor falls in love with his attractive protégée, as does one of his other students from America, Joe Schwartz. Joe is young, impatient, and brash; in short, all the things the professor is not. The two men, each supposing Felicité is in love with the other, decide to attempt a transmigration of souls with the aid of a new drug and the help of the cabalistic incantations of an ancient Hassidic sage. The strange experiment apparently works, for Joe becomes less arrogant, gentler, and more generous. The professor, in his turn, discovers a new energy and enthusiasm for his work. Felicité eventually marries Joe, and the two live successful and happy lives as scientists in California. Professor Buchhalter continues to contribute to the world of scientific discovery for many years.

The novella is interesting, not so much for its development of theme and character, but in its evocation of the mysterious and timeless qualities of the ancient city of Jerusalem. The city is pictured as haunting, yet beautiful—an exotic blend of the modern and the ancient: "Always in Jerusalem there is this sense of expectancy, this feeling that some new spark of meaning will appear and glow for an instant, and that it must be caught before it fades. And yet if the spark proves elusive one need not despair; surely the meaning will appear again, for in this place everything recurs. Even peace, too, hovers and fades and returns, uncertainly, shining for an interval, perhaps even a long interval, over this old-new city, Jerusalem."[16]

It is this transcendent vision of the biblical homeland that imbues much of Levin's Israeli novels with a unique quality. Unlike *The Settlers* and *The Harvest, The Spell of Time* does not intend to be a realistic work, but is rather a poetic fantasy. Like *My Father's House,* it is a symbolic story of Jewish life, revealing the more imaginative aspects of Levin's religious vision.

In choosing to write about Zionism—specifically, the theme of seeking one's Jewish identity in Israel—Levin stands virtually alone among American Jewish authors. American fiction about Israel, and by inference about the relationship of American Jews to Israel, is most noticeable through its absence. Levin is one of the few American authors who understood the significance of the land of Israel for the diaspora Jew. Levin's Israeli novels reflect his strong belief in the importance of Jewish identity and "continuity." "One doesn't dare destroy the continuity," Levin declared shortly after the publication of *The Settlers*, "doesn't dare give it up. . . . I think this is the central point in the Jewish psychology, the point that causes Jews to cling so long and so desperately, and sometimes with such terrible deprivations, to their identity as Jews."[17]

Ultimately it is Levin's ability to dramatically demonstrate the spiritual meaning of peoplehood that allows for his affirmative vision and renders much of his work memorable. Levin's portrayal of the events leading up to and culminating in the creation of the state of Israel remains one of his most lasting contributions to American Jewish letters. Perhaps even more significant has been his ability to translate into fiction the emotional and psychological importance, for Jews throughout the world, of the establishment of a national homeland.

Chapter Seven
Conclusion

The career of Meyer Levin was beset with an unusual number of problems: publication difficulties, litigations, personal disputes, and sheer bad luck. In response to a complaint from a woman who claimed she could be identified in *Reporter* (1929), Levin agreed to withdraw the novel soon after publication. *Yehuda* (1931) was the first American novel about Zionism and life in Palestine. But it appeared at the height of the depression, and salesmen reported that the title rendered the book unsaleable. *Citizens* appeared in 1940, just prior to the excitement of the preliminaries of war, and its reception was never enthusiastic. *Compulsion* (1956), although a great commercial success, was not without its litigation problems. There were distribution difficulties with his films, especially *The Illegals*, for which Levin had great hopes as a landmark document of the illegal flight of persecuted Jews to Palestine. Most frustrating of all were Levin's persistent troubles—including law suits, accusations, and personal attacks—concerning dramatic rights to *The Diary of Anne Frank*. Levin, who in large measure was responsible for the discovery and publication in English of *The Diary*, was commissioned to dramatize the book for stage production, only to have his play rejected by its producer. Later, a court ruled that the Broadway version was largely derivative from his original effort, and that he was entitled to receive fifty percent of the authors' royalties. Subsequent attempts, however, on Levin's part to stage his own play were blocked by the owners of the dramatic rights. The issue continued to preoccupy and frustrate him for nearly twenty years, culminating in the writing of *The Obsession*, Levin's version of the unfortunate incident.

In view of all this, it is not easy to evaluate Levin's true contribution to the literature of his time, or more specifically, his role in the development of American Jewish literature. Nor is it a simple matter to dismiss as mere paranoia his constant cry of "victimization" or his charge that he had been ignored because he was "too Jewish." It seems certain that Levin's contentious attitude, his ongoing legal difficulties, as well as his unabashed Zionism, did little to enhance his position with the literary establishment throughout much of his career.

With the publication of *The Old Bunch* in 1937, Levin was considered to be one of a small group of talented young Jewish writers, a group that included such authors as Daniel Fuchs, Henry Roth, and Mike Gold. After World War II, however, and the emergence of a new generation of Jewish writers and critics—authors such as Delmore Schwartz, Lionel Trilling, Saul Bellow, Irving Howe, Leslie Fiedler, Bernard Malamud, and Philip Roth—the writers of the 1930s seemed to fade quickly into the past and oblivion. Levin, a leftist like most of his early contemporaries, turned to Zionism and an exploration of Jewish themes and subjects in his fiction. His Jewish nationalism proved to be a particularly unfashionable position vis-à-vis the "universalist" thinking of the postwar generation of intellectuals. Saul Bellow's harsh judgment of Levin as "xenophobic" in his introduction to the first Dell edition of *Great Jewish Short Stories* (1963) serves to illustrate the general disregard for Levin's Zionistic views.[1]

There are, of course, several important factors to consider in evaluating Levin's career and the erosion of his popularity after World War II. To begin with, Levin's proletarian novels of the 1930s were very much in keeping with the mainstream of contemporary literature. More significantly, the works he produced during this period—*The New Bridge, The Old Bunch, Citizens*—were among the richest and the most imaginative of his career. Read today, *The Old Bunch* remains a highly creative and original work, the best of Levin's novels. His favorable reception during this time is partially attributable to the fact that his style and subject matter conformed to that of his peers. It is also true that his fiction of the 1930s was well conceived, and that his themes were important and carefully developed. By the 1960s his writing had lost much of its originality and vitality, as well as its relevance to the American social situation. *The Stronghold* had none of the structural innovations of *The Old Bunch, The Fanatic* none of the psychological fascination of *Compulsion.* The tense excitement generated throughout much of *Citizens* was not present in *Eva.* Moreover, the subjects and themes of these later works no longer seemed to strike at the heart of the collective imagination of the American people in general and American Jews in particular.

In short, the fiction that Meyer Levin wrote after 1960, while significant in some respects, does not seem well suited for the sophisticated tastes of the modern reader: his novels contain no refinement of point of view, no complex involutions of time, and few complicated characters that are capable of capturing our imagination. Too much of his later fiction appears to be a statement of the author's view of existence, rather than a rendering of experience.

This is not to say that Meyer Levin is an inconsequential writer. Throughout his career, Levin made notable contributions to American literature. As a writer of Jewish themes, he was one of the first to treat the American Jew as literary subject, and one of the first to explore the issues of assimilation and the crisis of identity. *The Old Bunch* remains an influential work, as well as one of the most memorable American Jewish novels of its decade.

Levin was also one of the first to understand the significance of the Zionist dream and to translate his affirmative vision of Palestine into literature. In 1931 Levin published *Yehuda*, the first novel about life in Palestine in the English language. That was followed in 1947 by *My Father's House.* In the 1970s, no longer feeling the need to participate in the mainstream of American literature, Levin wrote exclusively of Israel and its importance for Jews throughout the world. His literary domain was virtually his own, for few American Jewish writers in the 1960s and 1970s chose to deal with such subjects as the holocaust, the settlement of Palestine, or the modern state of Israel.

Finally, it must be said that Levin was not the great novelist he had once dreamed of becoming. Yet, although he may not have changed the course of American Jewish literature, he did indeed make a substantial contribution to its development. In a particularly candid moment of a self-analysis, Levin, in his autobiography, stated: "I may not be a Kafka or a Freud, but tradition flows in minor as well as in major creative spirits, the Jewish ways in the mind are deepened, and the material is carried onward; it is in this way that culture continues, and if I have done nothing else in my life than contribute an impulse to this stream, I am not lost."[2]

I would like to think that Levin is not "lost," that his "impulse" has been felt, for his works have heightened our insight and will continue to add to our understanding of a culture and a people.

Addendum

On 9 July 1981, as this book was being prepared for publication, Meyer Levin died of a stroke in Jerusalem. He was seventy-five years old and had just completed work on his sixteenth novel. *The Architect*, a documentary novel based on the life of Frank Lloyd Wright, was published in November 1981 by Simon and Schuster.

Levin had long been familiar with Wright and his work. In 1938 he published an article about the architect in *Coronet.* In the 1950s, a few years before Wright's death, Levin spent several months filming a number of Wright's buildings and talking with the architect himself. As was the case in many of his other experiences, these events eventually became the basis for a novel.

Levin believed Wright to be the first to create a distinctly American architectural style, one that was not derivative from European models. *The Architect* makes this point clearly and convincingly, and Levin is successful in representing Wright's ideas within the context of a fictional framework. He is also successful in recreating the Chicago of his youth, the city of *The Old Bunch,*

Citizens, and *Compulsion.* As in these earlier novels, historical figures (Clarence Darrow, Jane Addams, Harriet Monroe, Sandburg, Dreiser, and the young Hemingway) are intermingled with fictional characters. Levin is once again totally involved with his fictional milieu, writing of people and places he knows. As in some of his earlier documentary novels, Levin tends to sacrifice individual characterization for a wide view of social history. Yet as fiction that is close to fact, the novel is a lively and realistic account of a historical time and place; and unlike many of his earlier efforts, there is an appealing lightness of mood and tone in *The Architect.*

The Architect is not Levin's finest work. It is not, for example, the equal of *The Old Bunch.* Yet the novel once again demonstrates Levin's absorption with his craft and his ability to write of important and interesting themes. In reviewing *The Architect* in the *New York Times Book Review* (3 January 1982), Daniel Fuchs, one of Levin's early contemporaries, wrote movingly of Levin's more than fifty years of writing and concluded that Levin was "a man who took on the most painful themes of our times, who was on the scene throughout, and who worked to the limits of his strength in a long and honorable writer's career." *The Architect* is a fitting coda to Levin's very durable and fruitful career.

Notes and References

Chapter One

1. Meyer Levin, *In Search* (1950; reprint ed., New York, 1973), p. 6; all references are to the 1973 Pocket Books edition.
2. Harold U. Ribalow, "Zion in Contemporary Fiction," *Mid-Century,* ed. Harold U. Ribalow (New York, 1955), p. 572.
3. Meyer Levin, "Roosevelt Road: Three Chicago Sketches," *Menorah Journal* 10 (February 1924): 46.
4. Meyer Levin, "A Seder," *Menorah Journal* 10 (April 1924): 145.
5. *In Search,* p. 23.

Chapter Two

1. Meyer Levin, "The Writer and the Jewish Community," *Commentary* 3 (June 1947): p. 526.
2. *In Search,* p. 33.
3. Bernard Sherman, *The Invention of the Jew* (New York: Thomas Yoseloff, 1969), p. 99.
4. Ibid., p. 101.
5. Meyer Levin, *Reporter* (New York, 1929), p. 372.
6. Allen Guttmann, *The Jewish Writer in America* (New York, 1971), p. 12.
7. *In Search,* p. 30.
8. Ibid., p. 33.
9. Meyer Levin, *Frankie and Johnny* (New York, 1930), p. 29.
10. *In Search,* p. 46.
11. Ibid., p. 69.
12. Ibid., pp. 46–47.
13. Meyer Levin, *Yehuda* (New York, 1931), pp. 372–73.
14. For a more complete discussion of the history of Hassidism see Jerome R. Mintz, *Legends of the Hasidism* (Chicago: University of

Chicago Press, 1968) and Rabbi Dr. Harry Rabinowicz, *A Guide to Hassidism* (New York, 1960).

15. *In Search,* pp. 62–63.

16. Ibid., p. 63.

17. Meyer Levin, *The Golden Mountain* (New York, 1932), p. 4; reissued as *Classic Hassidic Tales* (New York, 1975). References are to the latter edition.

Chapter Three

1. *In Search,* p. 96.
2. Walter Rideout, *The Radical Novel in the United States* (Cambridge, 1956), p. 296.
3. David Madden, ed., *Proletarian Writers of the Thirties* (Carbondale, 1968), p. xxix.
4. Meyer Levin, *The New Bridge* (New York, 1933), p. 70.
5. *In Search,* p. 69.
6. Allen Guttmann, p. 39.
7. *In Search,* p. 72.
8. Marcus Klein, "The Roots of Radicals," in *Proletarian Writers of the Thirties,* p. 155.
9. Meyer Levin, *The Old Bunch* (1937; reprint ed., New York, 1970), p. 383; all references are to the 1970 Avon edition.
10. Daniel Walden, *On Being Jewish* (Greenwich, 1974), p. 157.
11. Marcus Klein, p. 156.
12. Allen Guttmann, p. 41.
13. Ibid., p. 44.
14. *In Search,* p. 93.
15. Ibid., p. 89.
16. Alfred Kazin, "The Jew as Modern American Writer," *Jewish American Literature*, ed. Abraham Chapman (New York: New American Library, 1974), p. 592.
17. *In Search,* p. 98.
18. Ibid., p. 99.
19. Ibid., p. 136.
20. Meyer Levin, *Citizens* (New York, 1940), p. 48.
21. Meyer Levin, "A Note on Method," in *Citizens,* p. 650.
22. *In Search,* pp. 137–38.

23. Chester E. Eisinger, "Character and Self in Fiction on the Left," *Proletarian Writers of the Thirties,* p. 170.

Chapter Four

1. *In Search,* p. 112.
2. Robert Gary's description of Levin is quoted by Evelyn Gendel, "The Successful Novelist and the Committed Jew," *Jewish Digest* 11 (July 1966):78.
3. Meyer Levin, *My Father's House* (New York, 1947), p. 14.
4. *In Search,* p. 345.
5. Ibid., p. 369.
6. Ibid.
7. Ibid., pp. 369–70.
8. Ibid., p. 369; references in this section hereafter cited in the text.
9. Jay David, *Growing Up Jewish* (New York, 1969), pp. 140–41.
10. Max Lerner, "Picaresque of Faith," *New Republic* 123 (23 July 1950):19.
11. Meyer Levin, *The Obsession* (New York, 1973), p. 34.
12. The citations from Thomas Mann and Albert Einstein are taken from the jacket cover of *In Search* (New York, 1973).
13. In *The Obsession* (pp. 271–72), Levin cites the following reviews: *Maariv (Evening)*: "In contrast with the much less dramatic version which was approved by Mr. Frank . . . Mr. Levin's version . . . is populated with living human beings instead of facsimiles." The *Jerusalem Post*: "It is on the whole a more honest dramatization than the slickly professional one we have seen before." *[illegible] (The Witness)*: "Infinitely superior to the Hackett version, which put aiming for a hit above faithfulness to the source." These same reviews are cited by Benno Weiser Varon, "The Haunting of Meyer Levin," *Midstream* 22 (August–September 1976):18.
14. Benno Weiser Varon, "The Haunting of Meyer Levin," p. 12.
15. Anne Frank, *The Diary of a Young Girl,* trans. B. M. Mooyaart (New York, 1952), p. 221.
16. *The Diary of Anne Frank,* dramatized by Frances Goodrich and Albert Hackett (New York, 1956), p. 168.
17. *In Search,* p. 20.
18. Ibid.
19. Ibid., p. 21.

20. *The Obsession,* p. 105.
21. Ibid., p. 104.
22. Meyer Levin, *Compulsion* (1956; reprint ed., New York, 1973), pp. 15–16; all references are to the 1973 Pocket Books edition.
23. Figures provided by Simon and Schuster, Inc.
24. *The Obsession,* p. 149.

Chapter Five

1. Rinna Dafni, "With Eva," *New York Times Book Review,* 23 August 1959, p. 4.
2. Meyer Levin, *Eva* (New York, 1959), p. 14.
3. Meyer Levin, *The Fanatic* (New York, 1963), p. 7.
4. Meyer Levin, *The Stronghold* (New York, 1965), p. 77.
5. Meyer Levin, *Gore and Igor* (New York, 1968), p. 11.
6. *Meyer Levin: Fifty Years in Writing,* (New York: Simon and Schuster, 1973), n.p. (Publicity pamphlet.)

Chapter Six

1. "I am a Jewish Writer," Interview with Arnold Forster, *ADL Bulletin,* March 1972, p. 4.
2. Interview with Phil Thomas, *AP Newsfeatures,* 10 May 1972.
3. "A Long Promise Kept," interview with Sidney Fields, *New York Daily News,* (20 April 1972), p. 74.
4. Arnold Forster, p. 4.
5. Meyer Levin, *The Settlers* (1972; reprint ed., New York, 1973), p. 3; all references are to the 1973 Pocket Books edition.
6. All sales figures cited were provided by the publicity department of Simon and Schuster, New York.
7. Meyer Levin, *The Obsession,* p. 216.
8. Interview with Phineas Stone, *The Jewish Week-American Examiner,* 12 March 1978, p. 30.
9. Meyer Levin, *The Harvest* (New York, 1978), p. 9.
10. Phineas Stone, p. 30.
11. Pearl K. Bell, "Meyer Levin's Obsessions," *Commentary* 65 (June 1978):68.
12. Harold U. Ribalow, "Zion in Contemporary Fiction," in *Mid-Century,* p. 572.

13. Meyer Levin, "Maurie Finds His Medium," *Menorah Journal* 15 (August 1928):178.

14. Ibid., p. 181.

15. Meyer Levin, "After All I Did For Israel," *Commentary* 12 (July 1951):62.

16. Meyer Levin, *The Spell of Time* (New York, 1974), p. 9.

17. Arnold Forster, p. 4 .

Chapter Seven

1. Saul Bellow, introduction, to *Great Jewish Short Stories,* ed. Saul Bellow (New York: Dell, 1963), as quoted in Benno Weiser Varon, "The Haunting of Meyer Levin," p. 13. Varon cites the following passage from the first Dell edition: "A curious surrender to xenophobia is concealed in this theorizing about art, and I am sure that Mr. Levin would not like to be identified with Oswald Spengler who is . . . an exponent of views of this sort. . . . Theories like Mr. Levin's . . . seldom bring any art into the world." Subsequent editions were edited to read: "Theories like those expressed by Mr. Levin's character, . . . seldom bring any art into the world" (Bellow, introduction, p. 15).

2. *In Search,* p. 347.

Selected Bibliography

PRIMARY SOURCES

1. Novels

The Architect. New York: Simon and Schuster, 1981.

Citizens. New York: Viking Press, 1940.

Compulsion. New York: Simon and Schuster, 1956. Reprint. New York: Pocket Books, 1958, 1973.

Eva. New York: Simon and Schuster, 1959.

The Fanatic. New York: Simon and Schuster, 1963.

Frankie and Johnny. New York: John Day, 1930. Reprint. *The Young Lovers.* New York: New American Library, 1952.

Gore and Igor. New York: Simon and Schuster, 1968.

The Harvest. New York: Simon and Schuster, 1978. Reprint. New York: Bantam, 1979.

My Father's House. New York: Viking Press, 1947.

The New Bridge. New York: Pat Covici, 1933.

The Old Bunch. New York: Simon and Schuster, 1937. Reprint. New York: Avon, 1970.

Reporter. New York: John Day, 1929.

The Settlers. New York: Simon and Schuster, 1972. Reprint. New York: Pocket Books, 1973.

The Spell of Time. New York: Praeger, 1974.

The Stronghold. New York: Simon and Schuster, 1965.

Yehuda. New York: Cape and Smith, 1931.

2. Autobiography

In Search. New York: Horizon Press, 1950. Reprint. New York: Pocket Books, 1973.

The Obsession. New York: Simon and Schuster, 1973.

3. Films

The Illegals. 1948.
My Father's House. 1947.
Voyage of The Unafraid. 1948.

4. Plays

Anne Frank. New York: Privately published by the author, n.d.
Compulsion, A Play. New York: Simon and Schuster, 1959.

5. Short Stories

"After All I Did For Israel." *Commentary* 12 (July 1951):57–62.
"A Seder." *Menorah Journal* 10 (April 1924):139–46.
"The Commune." *Menorah Journal* 19 (March 1931):297–304.
"How Satan Defeated Rabbi Israel in His Struggle Against The False Messiah: A Tale of the Baal Shem." *Menorah Journal* 20 (April 1932):21–25.
"Maurie Finds His Medium." *Menorah Journal* 15 (August 1928):175–81.
"Reb Feivel Read the Holy Books." *Menorah Journal* 18 (February 1930):129–35.
"Roosevelt Road: Three Chicago Sketches." *Menorah Journal* 10 (February 1924):46–51.

6. Nonfiction

An Israel Haggadah. New York: Behrman, 1968.
Classic Hassidic Tales. New York: Penguin Books, 1975. Reprint. *The Golden Mountain.* New York: Cape and Ballou, 1932. Reprint. New York: Behrman, 1951.
The Rise of American Jewish Literature. Edited by Charles Angoff and Meyer Levin. New York: Simon and Schuster, 1970.
The Story of Israel. New York: G. P. Putnam's Sons, 1967.

"What is an American Jewish Writer?" *Jewish Digest* 11 (May 1966): 31–34.

"The Writer and the Jewish Community." *Commentary* 3 (June 1947): 526–30.

SECONDARY SOURCES

Only those items of special interest or significance are listed. No full-length book analyses of Levin exist, and there are very few critical articles.

BELL, PEARL K. "Meyer Levin's Obsessions." *Commentary* 65 (June 1978): 66–68. Examines Levin's career as a whole with special emphasis on *The Harvest.*

BELLOW, SAUL. Introduction to *Great Jewish Short Stories,* edited by Saul Bellow. New York: Dell, 1963. Good general introduction to Jewish writing.

DAVID, JAY. *Growing Up Jewish.* New York: Morrow, 1969. Contains no specific information on Levin, but is excellent for background on Jewish immigrants and their children.

GENDEL, EVELYN. "The Successful Novelist and the Committed Jew." *Jewish Digest* 11 (July 1966):77–80. Retrospective analysis of Levin's career at sixty.

GUTTMANN, ALLEN. *The Jewish Writer in America.* New York: Oxford University Press, 1971. A study of the themes of assimilation and the crisis of identity from the beginning of American Jewish writing to the present. Contains a small section on Levin with a good analysis of *The Old Bunch* and some discussion of his earlier works.

KAZIN, ALFRED. "The Jew as Modern American Writer." In *The Commentary Reader*, edited by Norman Podhoretz. New York: American Jewish Committee, 1966. Some mention of Levin. Good discussion of the genesis of American Jewish writing.

MADDEN, DAVID, ed. *Proletarian Writers of the Thirties.* Carbondale: Southern Illinois University Press, 1968. Excellent collection of critical articles on the proletarian writers of the 1930s. Examination of *The Old Bunch* and some mention of *Citizens* in Marcus

Klein, "The Roots of Radicals," and Chester E. Eisenger, "Character and Self in Fiction on the Left."

MERSAND, JOSEPH. *Traditions in American Literature: A Study of Jewish Characters and Authors.* 1939. Reprint. Port Washington, N.Y.: Kennikat, 1968. Short discussion of Levin along with other Jewish writers of the early part of the century.

RABINOWICZ, RABBI DR. H. *A Guide to Hassidism.* New York: Thomas Yoseloff, 1960. History of Hassidism.

RIBALOW, HAROLD U. "Zion in Contemporary Fiction." In *Mid-Century,* edited by Harold U. Ribalow. New York: Beechhurst Press, 1955. Examines Jewish fiction dealing with the theme of Zionism and the state of Israel. Discusses Levin's early Zionist novels (*Yehuda* and *My Father's House*).

———. "A Note on Meyer Levin." *Chicago Jewish Forum* 9 (Fall 1950): 9–11. Short but interesting discussion of Levin's contribution to American Jewish literature.

RIDEOUT, WALTER. *The Radical Novel in the United States: 1900–1954.* Cambridge: Harvard University Press, 1956. Contains very little on Levin, but includes mention of *The New Bridge* and *Citizens* as "radical novels." Excellent study of leftist writers.

VARON, BENNO WEISER. "The Haunting of Meyer Levin." *Midstream* 22 (August–September 1976):7–23. Extensive discussion of Levin's involvement with *The Diary of a Young Girl* and the many personal and literary ramifications of that incident.

WALDEN, DANIEL, ed. *On Being Jewish.* Greenwich: Fawcett, 1974. Anthology of Jewish literature with an excellent introduction. Some mention of Levin and his contribution.

WEBER, BROM. "Some American Jewish Novelists." *Chicago Jewish Forum* 4 (Spring 1946): 179. Compares Levin to Dos Passos.

Index